language on display

Ladybirds
Lovely ladybirds, long legs lounging lazily on luscious leaves.

Frogs
Fast frogs hopping on frogspawn flicking furious flies from flowers.

Ladybirds
Lucky, lively ladybirds licking lemon lollies.

Frogs
Frolicking frogs flicking tongues to catch feathery flies.

Laura Collinson

Acknowledgements

The author and publishers would like to thank the children of Beaufort Primary School for the creative art work that has contributed to the making of this book.

Thanks to Di Anderson and Suzanne Kelly for their invaluable support and assistance.

Special thanks to Myra, Amy and Alice and to Sangida Khan for her outstanding artwork featured in many of the displays.

Finally, thank you to my husband Mike for all his patience and support.

This book is dedicated to my son George.

'Clay Tile Houses' (Page 59)

First published in 2003 by BELAIR PUBLICATIONS LIMITED
Albert House, Apex Business Centre, Boscombe Road, Dunstable, Beds LU5 4RL

© 2003 Folens on behalf of the author Laura Collinson

Commissioning Editor: Karen McCaffery   Editor: Elizabeth Miles
Design: Jane Conway   Photography: Kelvin Freeman   Cover design: Martin Cross

Illustrator: Jane Conway

Every effort has been made to contact copyright holders of material used in this book. If any have been overlooked, we will be pleased to make the necessary arrangements.

ISBN 0 947882 37 5

The cover photograph is taken from page 20.

Contents

Introduction

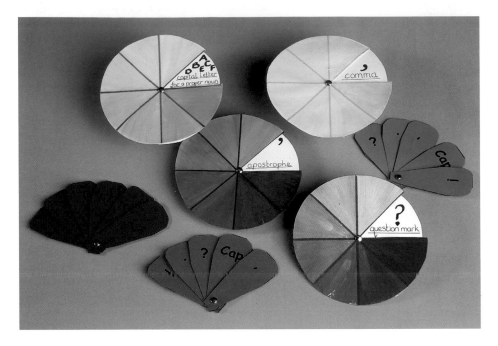

Language on Display is a book of creative and colourful ideas in which the 'World of Words' is enhanced through Art and Display.

A wealth of word, sentence and text level activities is provided, with ideas for spelling, grammar and punctuation and comprehension and composition, to help enrich the teaching of the English curriculum.

Many forms of grammar and punctuation are used in our writing to help us to communicate with other people.

Words help us to communicate, but choosing the right words and using them in an appropriate way is something that we have to learn. This is not an easy task as there are many different rules that apply when writing the English language, and just when we think we have completely understood a rule and can apply it to our writing, we discover that, in addition, there are exceptions that we must also understand and learn.

Words need punctuating in order to divide them up, accentuate them and understand them. Without punctuation, our writing would look very strange. For example:

withoutpunctuationwrittenenglishwouldlookverydifferenttherewouldbenofullstopsorspacestoseparatewords therewouldbenocapitallettersfornamesandplacesandwewouldnotknowwhenpeoplewerespeakingorwhenthey hadstoppedthewritingbecomesimpossibletoread

Games and Resources

Creative language games are an exciting way to present language concepts and consolidate learning. Ideas and suggestions are included for making useful games and resources such as punctuation wheels, show me fans, space bingo games and so on.

Language and Literature

The use of literature, poetry and non-fiction texts are featured strongly throughout the themes offered in this book. The recommended texts are used to model language, to entertain, stimulate imagination, broaden thinking skills and encourage reflection about the structures of language.

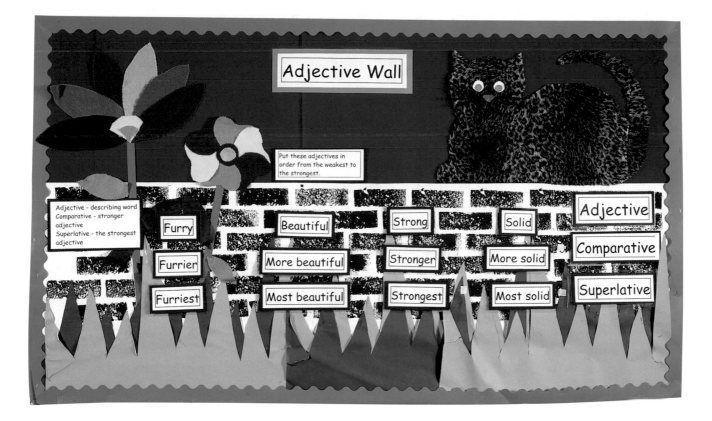

Language on Display

Language is an aid to creative thinking, as a means of oral and visual communication and expression. By displaying aspects of language in the classroom we can develop children's curiosity for the written word and foster their interest in reading and writing.

Good language displays can help children to:

- become interested in words and meanings
- develop a sense of purpose in their writing
- extend their bank of vocabulary
- develop questioning skills
- encourage the use of observational skills
- promote interactive involvement
- provide opportunities to share information
- view language in a wider aesthetic and visual context
- celebrate their achievements
- develop creativity in their knowledge and understanding of the uses of language.

Many of the displays featured in this book are interactive. They encourage the children to become part of the display, to move items and objects around and enable them to add their own ideas.

Because of their interactive nature, many of the labels, activities, resources and games shown in the displays have been laminated or covered in sticky back plastic for durability. This allows for many of the items to be re-used.

Children can be encouraged to make display labels and resources using a word-processing package. This makes the language clearer and easier to read and provides them with the opportunity to increase their knowledge and application of ICT skills.

Work that has been carefully mounted is also important in the creation of language displays. Whilst older children can be trained to cut and mount their own work for display, all children can contribute to display, through the selecting of work and choice of backing paper and labels. This all helps to foster their interest in the recording and presentation of their work.

I hope that through the ideas and images offered in this book, I have been able to provide suggestions for creating exciting and lively classroom environments in which children can develop their knowledge, understanding and enjoyment of language and art.

Laura Collinson

Hang Your Spellings Out to Dry

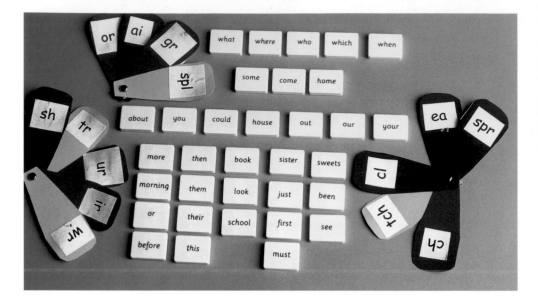

Language Activities

Blends – phonemes that have been combined into larger elements, such as clusters, syllables and words.

Spelling Blends

- Investigate the spelling of words with digraph blends where two letters represent one phoneme or sound, for example **ck**, and trigraph blends where three letters represent one phoneme or sound, for example **igh**. Think of as many words which include the blend as possible such as *clock, chick, shock, neck, truck, pick, speck, pack, lick* and illustrate them.
- Collect a variety of everyday objects that contain the **ck** blend. Match the objects to **ck** word cards such as *duck, chick, brick, truck, sock* and *clock*. Repeat for other blends.
- Write a list of words with other digraph blends such as,

ba**th**	**sh**ow	**ch**ur**ch**	su**ch**	**tr**ain	**tr**y	**gr**eat	**wor**d
hal**f**	**wor**k	**h**ead	**wor**ld	lea**ve**	**wr**ite	mo**th**	**wr**ong

- Read out the words together to see how they sound. For each word, highlight the two letters that represent one sound. (There may be more than one digraph in a word, such as **ch**ur**ch**, **tr**ain and **wr**ite.)
- Sort the words into columns of blends such as **th**, **ch**, **tr** and so on.
- Think of more words containing the blends to add to each list.

'Show Me' Cards

- Use 'Show Me' fan cards to practise blends. Read out a word with a particular blend to the children, for example **wrong**. The children then hold up the card in the fan that they think is correct such as **wr**. Ask the children to write the word with the correct spelling and underline the blend.

Spelling Spiders

- Create individual spelling spiders from coloured card and pipe-cleaners. Position a blend card, for example **ai**, in the centre of the spider's body. Laminate blank cards and place one at the end of each leg of the spider. Ask the children to write an **ai** word on each card and check the spelling with a dictionary. Repeat using different blends.

SOUnd it OUt

- Some words have common blends but different pronunciations, for example **ou** or **ear**. Introduce words with common spelling patterns but which sound different, for example *could*, *you* and *house*.
- Brainstorm as many words as possible with the **ou** spelling patterns and compare the words according to their sound for example:

ou	**oo**	**or**	**ow**
could	you	your	house
would		ought	about

Washing Line

- Use a washing line and a selection of individual letter and blend clothing cards to make words. Choose the blend to be practised and peg it to the centre of the washing line. Ask the children to position the clothes on the washing line to spell a word containing that blend.
- Repeat for the same blend but with new letter cards. Make a list of each new word created and say whether the blend is at the beginning, middle or end of the word. Check the spellings in a dictionary.
- Repeat for different blends.

Art and Display

Washing Lines

1. Make washing lines from three pieces of wood glued or nailed together or use commercially produced washing lines and pegs.
2. Draw clothing items onto coloured card and decorate them with colourful stickers. Laminate.
3. Add a selection of individual letters and blends to each item of clothing.
4. Peg the clothing items to the washing line to spell words.

Summer Daze

Compound Crossing

Language Activities

Compound words – words made up of two other words, such as *football*, *ladybird* and *sandcastle*.

Splitting Compounds

- Provide a list of compound words and identify how they are made up of more than one noun, for example *playground*, *cupboard*, *teapot*, *shoelace* and *wheelchair*.
- Ask the children to add to the list by collecting more examples of compound words. Practise splitting each word into its two component parts to help with spelling the whole word.

Garden Compounds

- Collect and list compound words that can be found in a country garden. Use information texts on animals, insects and plants for ideas. For example, *foxglove, bumblebee, greenhouse, dewdrop, bluebell, buttercup, hedgehog, ladybird, dragonfly and rainbow*.
- Draw a picture to illustrate each word found.
- Split each compound word into its two component nouns and print onto card.
- Change the positioning of each component in the compound word, for example, *ladybird* becomes *birdlady*. Discuss the effect that this has on the meaning of the new word.

Crossing Compounds

- Cross two compound words and explore the different combinations of words that you can achieve, for example: What do you get if you cross a ladybird with a dragonfly? *A dragonbird*.
- Other combinations could include *ladydragon*, *dragonlady*, *ladyfly* or *flybird*. Illustrate your chosen answer.

Compound Word Inventor

- Use your compound words listed to create new and imaginary compound words, for example *butterfly = symmetry-bug; greenhouse = emerald-residence*. Use hyphens when the words become lengthy in order to read each part clearly.

8

Art and Display

Flowers

1. Paint pictures of flowers using very thick finger paint or PVA glue mixed with poster paint.
2. Draw flowers in fine detail onto fabric such as coloured felt. Cut out and apply beads and colourful threads for details of any markings on the petals.
3. Using items such as tissue paper, pipe-cleaners, egg cartons, crêpe paper, cardboard tubes, beads and sequins, create a variety of 3D flowers with compound names (for example: *bluebell*, *sunflower*, *foxglove* and *honeysuckle*).

Butterflies

1. Fold a piece of card in half and splatter poster paint in a combination of colours onto one side. Fold the card in half again and gently press down, then open the two halves to reveal a symmetrical pattern on both sides.
2. When dry, cut into butterfly shapes and attach to a mobile or use as a background for writing.
3. Alternatively, marble white card in a variety of coloured inks and cut into butterfly shapes when dry.
4. Decorate butterflies with large sequins or butterfly clips and add curled pipe-cleaners for antennae.

Ladybirds

1. Make two red pom-poms and stick them together to create a body.
2. Glue tiny black pom-poms or felt spots to the back of the ladybird.
3. Cut out a circular face from black felt material and glue on two eyes. Attach the face to the body.

Bees

1. Use a cardboard tube to create the body of a bee. Fill the ends of the tube with black tissue paper.
2. Paint the tube in black and yellow stripes or cover in tissue paper.
3. Add pipe-cleaner antennae and beads for eyes and suspend on string from a covered hoop.

Dragonflies

1. Fold strips of coloured felt around a rectangular shaped body.
2. Create wings from thin modelling wire with coloured net wrapped around them. Attach them to the body.
3. Decorate the body and the wings with large sequins and attach coloured pipe-cleaners for legs.

Compounded in Space

Language Activities

Compound words – words made up of two other words, such as *spaceship*, *handbag* and *iceberg*.

Lunar Brainstorm

- Brainstorm words or nouns associated with space. For example, *moon*, *rocket*, *space*, *star*, *scientist*, *landing* and *planet*.

- Use these words as a basis for building other space related words that are made up of more than one noun, for example *spaceman, starlight, moonlight, moonbeam, spaceship* and *spacesuit*.

Compound Word Matching

- From the compound space words identified, print cards with the words split into their two component parts. For example *space* and *man*.
- Mix up the cards and match them to create compound space words.

Position of Space

- Look at the list of compound space words and work out how many times the word 'space' can be used as the first and the second component of a compound word.

Spaced-out Sentences

- Make up space sentences that include two or more compound words. For example:

  The **spaceman** landed the **spacecraft** before exploring the lunar **landscape**, as thousands of shooting stars lit up the **moonscape**.

Space Bingo

- Create several different Space Bingo baseboards with three columns and four rows. Write an individual noun from the compound words into each space on the board. Each baseboard should create six compound words.
- Provide each child with a baseboard and from the compound word bank randomly call out each compound space word. When the children hear a noun that is written on their card, they can cover the word with a coloured counter. Cover the partner noun with the same colour counter when it is called out.
- The winner is the first to cover the whole card with compound nouns and read them out correctly.

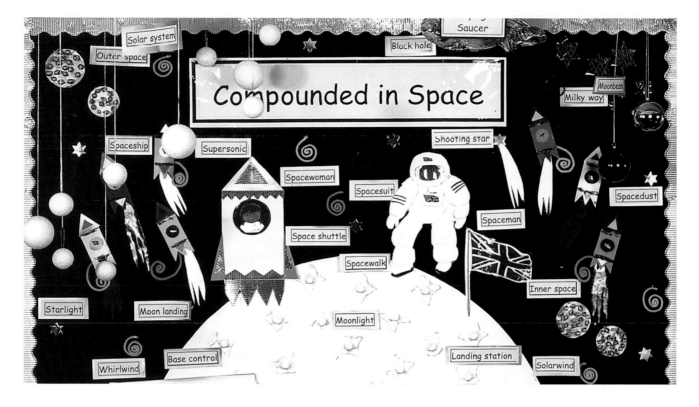

Art and Display

Lunar Landscape

1. On a black background create a lunar landscape with a large white moon.
2. Cut out a hemisphere of white card and glue on squashed egg containers. Paint white.

Spaceman

1. Make an astronaut from thick white felt. Cut out shin pads, kneepads and boots and glue on top to give a 3D relief.
2. Add stripes to the sleeves and a flag to the chest of the spacesuit. Cover with transparent self-adhesive film.
3. Use a computer draw package to draw a face for the astronaut. Cut out a small circle of acetate and glue the face to the back of it. Cover with a helmet made from thick white felt with a window cut out for the face.

Spaceship

1. Cover a large sponge ball in silver baking foil.
2. Cut out a large circle of card, remove the centre so that the ball can fit into it and cover in silver baking foil.
3. Add sequins to the ball to represent a large spaceship.

Solar System

1. Paint, spray or add glitter to polystyrene balls to create a solar system, moonbeams and planets.
2. Make pasta planets by gluing pasta shapes to circles of card. Spray with gold and silver paint.
3. Cover a large hoop in silver and white crêpe paper and suspend the planets from the hoop with silver thread.

Shooting Stars and Whirlwinds

1. Glue silver stars to the display board and add metallic crêpe paper to represent flames for shooting stars.
2. Coil coloured pipe-cleaners directly on to the display board to create whirlwinds.

Rockets

1. Make card cutouts of rockets from flat card, or use cardboard tubes for a 3D effect.
2. Decorate the rockets with paper, glitter, sequins and pipe-cleaners. Glue a small international flag on each.
3. Add metallic crêpe paper to represent flames on the tail of the rockets.

Robotic Consolidator

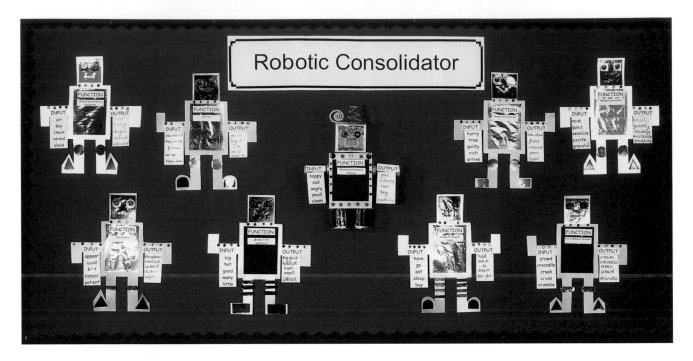

Language Activities

Antonyms – words which are opposite in meaning to other words, such as *light* and *dark*, *deep* and *shallow*, *tall* and *short*.

Opposites

- Call out a variety of words for the children to write the opposites or antonym. For example *hot, light, big, full, winter, fast, open, night, cold, sour, right, tall, soft, out, poor, smooth, warm, up*.
- Explore if more than one antonym can be found for each word, such as *big – small/tiny/little*.

Opposite Bingo

- Make several bingo cards printed with words that have opposites.
- Randomly call out a range of antonyms and ask the children to cover the opposite of that word with a counter on their card.
- The winner is the first to cover the whole card with counters.
- Check the answers by asking the winner to reveal each word in turn, calling out its antonym.

Opposite Stories

- Read a simple story with the children and highlight words and phrases that could be changed to antonyms.
- Rewrite the story together, substituting the words and phrases for appropriate antonyms.
- Write short simple stories and exchange them with a partner to rewrite and compose the opposite story.

Antonym Prefixes

- Use the prefixes *un-, in-, im-, and dis-* to generate antonyms from root words, such as *happy, decision, possible, honest, comfortable, correct, perfect, agree* and so on.
- Work in pairs with a dictionary to make a list of antonyms beginning with the above prefixes.
- Write down the definition for each antonym.
- Identify the root word for each antonym and write the word in a sentence. Discuss how the prefix changes the meaning of the root word.
- Repeat the activity using *il-, ir-* and *non-*.

Function Machines

- Make function machines to practise work on antonyms. Provide the function, for example *change the input to an antonym* and the input words, such as *soft* or *right*, and ask the children to think of the output (*hard* or *left*).
- Alternatively, provide the function and the output and ask the children to provide the input words or provide the input and output words and ask the children to provide the function.
- Provide the function only and ask for as many input and output words as possible.

Art and Display

2D Robot Function Machine

1. Cut out robot shapes from silver or gold card.
2. Provide a range of metallic paper, buttons, beads, gold spray, glitter, sequins and other metallic materials to decorate the robots.

3D Robot Function Machine

1. Create 3D robots using cardboard tubes, boxes, egg cartons and string. Use a large box for the body, a small box for the head and four card tubes for the arms and legs.
2. Make several small cuts into the card tubes at each end, approximately 2cm in from the edge. Fold back and glue into place on the body.

Function Cards

1. Create Input, Function and Output cards. Attach these to the chest and arms of the robots with double-sided Velcro.
2. Laminate blank Input and Output cards for the children to write on. These can then be erased and used again for different functions.

Function cards can also be made for practising:

- Singular words to plurals
- Nouns to verbs
- Verbs to nouns
- Past tense verbs to present tense verbs
- Verbs to adverbs
- Homophones
- Synonyms
- Suffixes

Some Pig

Language Activities

Synonyms – words that have the same or a similar meaning as another word, such as *wet* and *damp*, *ill* and *sick*, *happy* and *joyful*.

Synonyms

- Provide a variety of high frequency words suitable for generating plenty of synonyms. Ask the children to find as many words that mean the same as the start word. For example, *little, big, good, nice, nasty, happy, sad, pretty, friendly*.
- Use a thesaurus as well as the computer thesaurus to add to the list.
- Make a class thesaurus of the children's synonyms generated for high frequency words and use for reference when writing.

Synonym Shades

- Provide lists of synonyms which have similar meanings, such as:

  Hot, warm, tepid, boiling, scorching, lukewarm, blistering, sizzling.

Cold, cool, icy, chilly, freezing, frosty, bitter, wintry.
Frightening, scary, unreal, terrifying, spooky, startling, alarming.
Happy, joyful, contented, glad, pleased, cheerful.

- Order and discuss each set of words according to their intensity or shades of meaning. For example:

  Lukewarm, tepid, warm, hot, boiling, scorching, sizzling, blistering.

Character Synonyms

- Use a class book such as *Charlotte's Web* by E.B. White (Puffin Books, 1963) as a starting point for discussing character descriptions.
- Make a list of adjectives that are used to describe each character in the story.
- Use a thesaurus to find as many synonyms as possible to describe each character.
- Copy and enlarge a picture of a chosen character from the story and write all the synonyms in the middle of the character's body.

Something Else was 'Said'

- Use one chapter of the book to collect the synonyms that are used in dialogue in place of the word 'said'. For example *squealed, yelled, sobbed, gaggled, shouted, sniffed, whispered, cried*.
- Identify which synonyms are used the most and the least to replace 'said'.
- Write a paragraph from the book replacing all words used in dialogue that represent the word 'said' with a suitable alternative from those collected.

Synonym Stories

- Write a short story for a partner to read. Underline the words that you would like to be changed and ask your partner to find the best, most appropriate synonym to add interest to your writing. For example:

My dog is a ***good*** dog. He ***loves*** going out for a ***walk*** twice a day. The ***trouble*** is that he even wants to go out when it's ***pouring*** down with rain. When we ***come*** back from our walk, my mum goes ***mad*** when she sees the ***mess*** in the hall and on the kitchen floor. Even though I ***try*** to ***clear*** it up before she sees, my dog makes it ***filthy*** again by ***shaking*** all over.

My dog is a ***well-behaved*** dog. He ***enjoys*** going out for a ***stroll*** twice a day. The ***problem*** is that he even wants to go out when it's ***teaming*** down with rain. When we ***arrive*** back from our walk, my mum goes ***crazy*** when she sees the ***untidiness*** in the hall and on the kitchen floor. Even though I ***attempt*** to ***tidy*** it up before she sees, my dog makes it ***grimy*** again by ***quivering*** all over.

Art and Display

Some Pig

1. Draw or photocopy the outline of a character from your chosen book.
2. Transfer the drawing onto an overhead projector and enlarge onto coloured card or paper.
3. Write the lists of synonyms to describe your character in large, clear writing, in the middle of the image.
4. Provide other material related to the character to add to the display. For example, hay for Wilbur to sit on, a magic wand for Harry Potter to hold, or perhaps a book for Matilda.
5. Construct 'Think' or 'Speech' bubbles using ICT. Inside the bubbles provide suggestions and open-ended questions for the children to consider.

Dictionary Dash

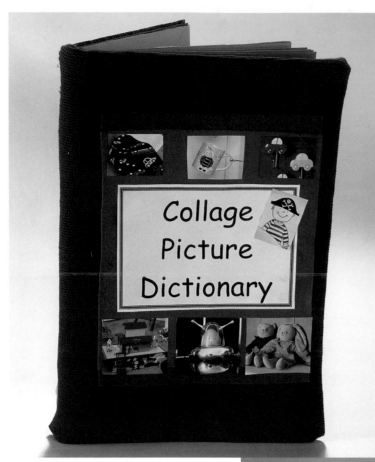

Language Activities

Alphabet Revision

- Recite the alphabet forwards and backwards for practise.
- Sing alphabet rhymes and songs.
- Ask questions such as: Which letter comes after 'p', 'n', 'f'? What is the third, fourth and fifth letter after the following letters: 'c', 'g', 'o'?

Collage Dictionary

- In a large scrapbook, label the top of each page with each letter of the alphabet.
- Cut pictures from magazines beginning with each letter of the alphabet and glue on to the appropriate pages.
- Write a list of the objects that you see on each page in alphabetical order.

Alphabetical Objects

- Provide a range of everyday objects such as a pencil, ruler, book, cup, teapot and a stapler. Ask the children to arrange the objects in an alphabetical line.
- Add more objects to the list, including several which begin with the same letter. For example a plant, pot, pine cone, pencil and paper. Extend to include objects to be sequenced by third and fourth place letters.

Picture Dictionaries

- Illustrate and write simple definitions of the words from Alphabetical Objects to make a class picture dictionary.
- Design and make a picture dictionary of topic words or significant words of personal interest to the children. Include illustrations and simple definitions of each word.

Write the objects that you see in alphabetical order. Add more pictures to each page of the dictionary.

Dictionary Split

- Play Dictionary Split. Each child has a dictionary and is challenged within a group or the class to open or split the dictionary at the right letter for any given word.
- Before finding each word discuss whether the word will be at the beginning, middle or end of the dictionary. Continue in order to build up speed and accuracy.

Beat the Timer

- Provide a set of words to be organised in alphabetical order using second place letters. For example:

  creative, circular, century, candles, colour, custard.

- Work with a partner and using a timer, see who can write the words in the correct order in the quickest time.
- Repeat the activity for third and fourth place letters.

Art and Display

Everything in Good Order

1. Make a large interactive dictionary that has removable words and activities.
2. Cover a large scrapbook with bright, attractive paper.
3. On every other page, cut slits down the centre approximately 5cm apart and approximately 20cm in length, using a craft knife. Place a thick piece of card beneath the page when cutting so that the cuts do not break on to the next page.
4. With a pencil, draw through each slit so the pencil line appears on the page behind and glue a line approximately 4cm below each pencil mark.
5. Glue around the border of the page and stick the two pages together. You should be left with a page of cuts just deep enough to place cards into so that they show at the top and do not fall too far below.
6. The first page should contain a variety of words all beginning with the letter 'a'. These could be topic related words or high frequency words.
7. Glue explanations of activities and games to play on each facing page, such as Dictionary Split and Beat the Timer.

Delightful Words

Language Activities

Root words – words to which prefixes and suffixes may be added to make other words.

Root Words

- Use a root word such as *clear* to demonstrate how new words can be generated by adding a variety of prefixes and suffixes. For example, *clearly, **un**clear, clear**ed**, clear**ing***.
- Provide a range of words to which the prefixes *al-* and *a-* can be added. For example, *mighty, most, pine, so, ready, ways, like, cross, light, head, ground, float, sleep, live, lone, shore, stray, loft, loud* and so on.
- Find the meanings of each word in the dictionary and ask the children to work out what the meanings of the prefixes *al-* and *a-* are.
- Supply each child with a suffix fan illustrating the suffixes *-en, -ly, -ful, -less*. Provide a variety of words such as *bright, colour, soft, quiet, truth, proud, hard, calm* and *hope*, and ask the children to display the appropriate suffix/es that can be added to each word.
- Suggest how they influence the meanings of the words and write out each new word in a complete sentence.

Verbs and Nouns

- Explore how root words can be changed from a verb to a noun by adding the suffix *-er*. Provide the children with a variety of verbs and ask them to change them to nouns. For example *sing, dance, clean, dust, walk, fight, paint, plumb, teach, speak, play*.
- Examine those words which change their spelling after the suffix *-er* is added. For example *writer, joker, shopper, runner, jogger, juggler* and so on. Identify any spelling patterns and add more words to each list.
- Discover how root words can be changed from the present tense to the past tense by adding the suffix *-ed*. Provide a list of present tense verbs and ask the children to change them into the past tense, for example *paint, walk, clean, climb, heat, play, talk, lick, pick, fasten*.
- Investigate the effect of changing singular words to the plural by adding the suffix *-s* to the end of each word. Discuss the plural spelling of words ending in *y* such as *baby, lady, cherry, berry, puppy, dictionary* and words like *sheep, children* and *mouse*. Make a die with plural endings *-s, -es* and *-ies*. Roll the die and write a plural verb with the ending shown on the die.

In Lightning Time

- In pairs, generate as many derivations as possible from the root word *light*. Set a time limit of five minutes. Provide dictionaries for extra help.

Lightning	Flight
Delight	Lighter
Enlighten	Lighten
Slight	Lights
Slightly	Lightened
Alight	Light-headed
Lightweight	Relight
Delightful	Flighty
Lighthouse	Nightlight
Light-switch	

- Identify those words that have been made using a prefix or a suffix, and which ones can now be called a compound word.
- Write a list of the common prefixes and suffixes that have been added to the word *light,* for example *de-, en-, a-, re-, -en, -ly, -ful, -er, -s*, and consider how the meaning of the root word may have changed.

Art and Display

Translucent Tissue Candles

1. Open up a large white plastic bin liner and spread it out flat on a tabletop.
2. Using a large brush, spread a mixture of 40% PVA glue and 60% water all over the surface of the white plastic.
3. Apply strips of coloured tissue paper to the entire surface of the liner, overlapping to create new colours.
4. Spread another layer of glue mixture on top of the tissue and leave to dry.
5. When dry, peel the layer of coloured tissue from the liner.
6. Cut the paper into a variety of candle shapes and cut out shapes to represent flames. Glue the flames to the top of each candle.
7. Use sequins, shiny ribbon and beads to decorate the candles.
8. Display the candles on windows alongside a variety of *light* words.

Clay Diwas (oil lamps)

1. Roll a piece of terracotta clay into a large ball. Press both thumbs into the clay, pushing against the sides to create the walls of the pot. Make a small spout at one end by pinching the clay into a triangular shape between the thumb and forefinger.
2. Place a small mosaic tile in the bottom of each pot and fire in a kiln. The tile will melt in the bottom of the diwa leaving a shiny colourful base.
3. Spray the pot inside and out using silver or gold spray paint.
4. Glue on small mirror tiles to the insides of the pot for an extra special effect when the candles are lit.
5. These pots can be made using self-drying clay if a kiln is unavailable. If so, do not add the mosaic tiles to these pots.

⚠ **Safety Note: When lighting the diwas, always follow the fire procedures for your school.**

A Stitch in Time

Language Activities

Idioms – sayings or phrases, the words of which are not meant literally, for example '*over the moon*'.

Idioms

- Make a list of idioms to share with the children. For example: *over the moon, under the weather, turn over a new leaf, smell a rat, blow your own trumpet, get into hot water, have a bee in your bonnet, let the cat out of the bag, jump the gun, sit on the fence, burn the candle at both ends* and so on.
- Ask the children to provide their own explanations of their meanings.
- Explain what they do not mean and use dictionaries to research their actual meanings and origins.
- Make a book of idioms and illustrate them literally as they are written. Provide the real meanings alongside.

Proverbs

Proverbs – sayings that state a belief about the world, for example '*the early bird catches the worm*'.

- Collect well-known proverbs such as: *An apple a day keeps the doctor away, Too many cooks spoil the broth, The grass is always greener on the other side, A stitch in time saves nine, Absence makes the heart grow fonder, When the cat's away the mice do play, Out of the frying pan into the fire, Two heads are better than one, No news is good news, Look after the pennies and the pounds will look after themselves, More haste less speed, The early bird catches the worm, Better late than never, First come first served, Early to bed early to rise.*
- Ask the children to explore the possible meanings of each proverb and research their actual meanings and origins using a dictionary.
- Choose one proverb to illustrate.

Catch-Phrase

- Choose a favourite proverb or idiom to illustrate as a line drawing. Copy the illustration onto an overhead transparency and ask the children to guess what 'catch-phrase' the illustration depicts.
- Repeat the activity for each child's illustrated catch-phrase.

Time and Time Again

- Collect as many sayings and phrases that include the word 'Time' or refer to time. For example: *Time and tide wait for no man, Time is of the essence, A stitch in time saves nine, Time heals old wounds, Time is a great healer.*
- Ask the children to suggest possible meanings for each of the sayings and to sort them into idioms and proverbs.
- Draw a large clock and write an idiom or proverb about time around the clock face.
- Research the origins of the idioms and proverbs using dictionaries.
- Write sentences accurately, using the idioms and proverbs, for example: *I kept putting off doing my homework, but my Mum said, "There's no time like the present. You don't want to rush it before school starts tomorrow morning, do you?"*

Art and Display

2-Dimensional Clock

1. Using a variety of coloured card, cut out the outline of a clock.
2. Create a computer generated clock face and glue to the middle of the clock.
3. Write a time related idiom or proverb around the clock face in large, clear handwriting.
4. Add gummed geometric shapes to the border of the clock for decoration.

3-Dimensional Clock

Note: A working clock mechanism and batteries are required for making this clock.

1. To make a 3-dimensional clock, use strips of thick grey card to make a strong, open-ended box on which to position the clock face. Make a second open-ended rectangular box for the base of the clock.
2. Secure the two boxes together with masking tape and cut out a triangular section of card for the top of the clock. Secure with masking tape too.
3. Prepare a mixture of PVA glue and water and, using small strips of plain white paper, papier mâché the entire clock framework three times and leave to dry.
4. Use oil-based paint in one colour to cover the framework of the clock and leave it to dry overnight.
5. Use a bradawl or a small drill to make a hole in the centre of the clock through which the clock mechanism will fit.
6. Decorate the clock with bright coloured foil, card, paper and gummed shapes.
7. Varnish the clock with a weak solution of PVA glue and water.
8. When the clock is completely dry, insert the clock mechanism through the base of the framework and fasten securely in place.

I Say, I Say, I Say ...

Language Activities

Question mark (?) – punctuation mark used at the end of a sentence to denote a question.

Question Marks

- Read fact finding books containing a range of questions and answers such as *1000 Questions and Answers* by Nicola Baxter (Bookmart, 2001) to identify question openers.
- Note how each subheading begins with a question which is then answered in the paragraph that follows. Identify the most common question openers used in preparation for your own writing.
- Copy a page from the book and delete the question marks. Place a transparent sheet of paper over the page and ask the children to decide where the question marks should be. Repeat this activity for several different pages.
- Ask the children to identify and list questions encountered in their own reading books. Compare the different variety of questions collected and for what purpose they are asked, for example: *asking for help, asking the time, asking someone to be quiet* and so on.

Wh Words

- Identify the words that questions most commonly open with, for example words beginning with the blend **wh** such as *who, what, why, where, when, which.*
- Provide a series of questions with the opening word deleted such as *time is lunch, do you think you are going, will you be finished playing, are you always nasty to me, jacket do you prefer.*
- Complete the sentences by adding the appropriate opening word and finishing with a question mark.

Question Openers

- Explore other opening words for questions such as *can, do, have, may, will, would, could, should.*
- Write a question for each of these opening words. Challenge children to write questions where the question word is written in the middle of the sentence such as *Since it poured with rain yesterday, can we go to the park today?*

Fact Finders

- Ask the children to make a list of questions about a subject of their choice using a variety of question openers. For example a science theme such as materials – *Which materials conduct electricity? How many materials can be used as insulators?*
- Make a Fact Finders book containing the questions to be researched and pictures of the subject. Decide whether or not to include the answers.

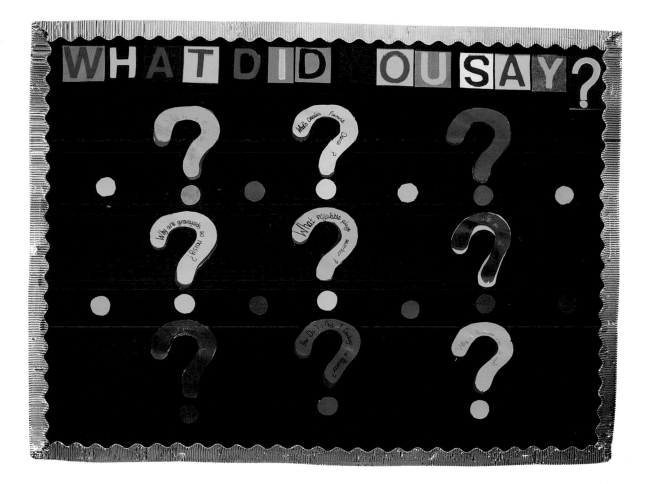

Jokes

- Read out 'I say' jokes and discuss how voice tone changes when a joke question is being read. The voice can go up or down at the end of the question. Try it both ways. Which way sounds best?
- In pairs make up 'I say' jokes remembering to use the correct punctuation.

Current Issues

- Look at a variety of questionnaires and consumer survey sheets. Pay particular attention to the way that questions are presented.
- Design your own questionnaire to be completed by other children on a whole school issue such as the toilet facilities, lunchtime supervision and playground equipment.
- Evaluate the answers given from the questionnaire and write statements based on those facilities that have been recognised as good and statements explaining what you will do to improve the facilities which need developing.

Art and Display

What Did You Say?

1. Use 'I say' jokes to create an interactive question display.
2. Use the computer to print out a very large question mark.
3. Photocopy the question mark onto card and cut it out to use as a stencil.
4. Use the stencil to draw and cut out two question marks on coloured card for each child.
5. In large clear handwriting write the joke question on one question mark and write the statement answer on the other.
6. Position one question mark on top of the other so that you read the question and lift up the top question mark to reveal the answer below.
7. Glue the two together along the top arch of the question mark.
8. Inter-space the question mark jokes with colourful full stops on the display board.
9. Create a display title using brightly coloured cutout letters mounted on squares of contrasting colours.

Punctuation Palette

Language Activities

Punctuation – a way of marking written text to help readers' understanding. The most commonly used marks in English are the apostrophe, colon, comma, dash, ellipsis, exclamation mark, hyphen, question mark, semi-colon, speech mark.

Commas

Comma – punctuation mark marking the relationship between parts of a sentence, or used to separate items in a list.

List Line-up

- Choose five children to stand in a line. Ask the children to say their first names one after the other without taking a breath between each of them.
- Give large comma cards to three children and a 'and' card to another child.
- Ask the children with the comma cards to stand in the line with the five named children in a position where they think the commas should be placed and the child with the 'and' card to stand in the correct position.
- Read the sentence again, taking a breath where the comma cards are positioned.

A Wish List

- Provide catalogues that contain pictures of children's items and toys.
- Ask the children to create a 'Wish List' by cutting out photographs of items that they would like.
- Arrange the pictures in a line, perhaps as a concertina zigzag book, writing a comma between each item and the word 'and' before the last item in the list.
- Write out the sentence, replacing the pictures with words.

Write a List

- Provide a variety of topics to practise list-making, such as a journey, in my bedroom, at the seaside, in the orchestra and so on.
- Choose one of the topics and ask the children to write a list using commas and the word 'and', for example: *For my journey I will need to take a sleeping bag, a pair of boots, a tent, a torch and a compass.*

Pyramid Lists

- Use a computer word package to generate a pyramid list of items with commas and the word 'and' by centring each new line of text, for example:

At the seaside you can find

shells.
shells and seaweed.
shells, seaweed and sand.
shells, seaweed, sand and seagulls.
shells, seaweed, sand, seagulls and starfish.

Commas for Clauses

- Write a sentence which includes a clause such as:

  She looked out of the window which was opened wide to see the cat at the top of the tree.

- Discuss how the sentence is difficult to say without taking a breath. Ask the children where they think the commas should be placed and to rewrite the sentence.
- Rewrite the sentence removing the clause 'which was opened wide' and ask the children if the sentence still makes sense. Explain how the clause improves the sentence.
- Repeat the activity for different sentences and clauses.
- Use classic texts to search for commas which identify clauses within sentences. Write each sentence without the clause to see if it makes sense.

Apostrophes for Contractions

Apostrophe – punctuation mark indicating a contraction when two words are shortened into one. The apostrophe is placed where letters have been dropped, for example: *it's, I'm, we've, didn't*.

Contractions

- Write a list of words which have been contracted such as *don't, won't, shouldn't, she'll, I'll, he'd, they've, we've*. Ask the children to say what they notice about each word and write the words out in their full form.
- Generate a list of words which can be contracted such as *would not, can not, has not, you would, they will, we have*, and ask the children to write the words in their contracted form using an apostrophe.

Fishing for Contractions

- Print words onto fish-shaped cards that together can be contracted. On the back of each card attach a self-adhesive magnet. Make fishing lines from straws and string and tie a magnet to the end of the string.
- Place the fish cards on a paper pond and using the fishing rod, catch two fish cards that together can be contracted. Write the words as a contraction.
- Ask the children to write their contracted words in a sentence. For example: *They'll be arriving at seven thirty this evening.*

25

Apostrophes for Possession

Apostrophe – punctuation mark indicating possession.

With a singular noun or collective noun, the apostrophe is added before the 's', for example: *the cat's tail, the children's work*. When a plural is marked by 's', the apostrophe is added after the 's' as in *the cats' tails*.

Title Time

- Make a collection of books, magazines and comics with titles that contain an apostrophe to show possession. For example, *The Lighthouse Keeper's Lunch, Billy's Beetle, Carrie's War, Woman's Weekly, Reader's Digest*.
- Identify the subject and object of each book title by asking questions such as 'Who does the lunch belong to?', 'Whose beetle was it?'

Whose Object?

- Sit the children in a circle with one object that belongs to them. For example, Joanne has a calculator.
- Ask each child in turn to stand up and make a statement about their object. Explain that there is one person, *Joanne,* and one object, *the calculator*, and the calculator belongs to Joanne therefore it is *Joanne's calculator*.
- Model how to write this using an apostrophe to show belonging. Ask the children to write a statement showing the possessive apostrophe for each person's object.

Supermarket Sweep

- Visit a local supermarket and make a list of food items with apostrophes in the brand name, such as *Sharwood's Lime Pickle, Cadbury's Chocolate, Johnson's Baby Wipes, Fox's Crunch Creams, Carr's Water Biscuits* and *Kellogg's Cornflakes*.
- Make a collection of boxes and wrappers from the items and ask the children to write a sentence which includes one item from the display such as:

  Would you like a Cadbury's Finger with your tea?

Possessive Plurals

- Make a list of plural subjects that end in the letter 's' such as *parents*, *dogs*, *teachers* and *babies*. Demonstrate how to add an apostrophe after the last letter of each subject to show that more than one subject owns the object/s. For example, the *babies' nursery* shows that the nursery belongs to many babies.
- Using your list of plural subjects write a sentence using a possessive apostrophe to show that each subject owns an object/s collectively.

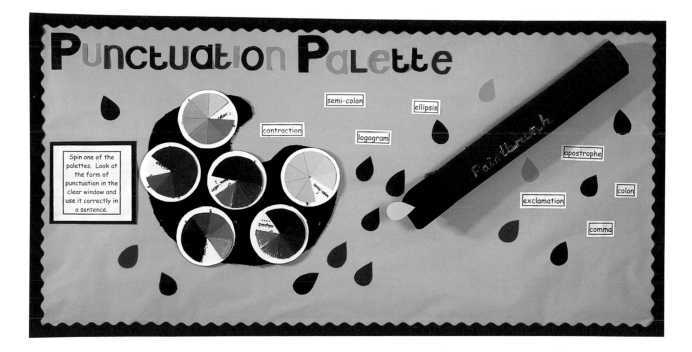

Show Me – Punctuation Fans

- Make punctuation fans by printing the different forms of punctuation such as question marks, full stops, capital letters, commas and apostrophes onto coloured card. Arrange them together to make a punctuation fan joined at the centre with a paper fastener.
- Provide the children with unpunctuated sentences and ask them to identify the missing punctuation and hold up the fan to show the appropriate punctuation card for each sentence. For example:

What do you think of the weather today
I like sweets chocolate lollipops and ice cream
Marys glasses help her to read

Punctuation Wheels

- Use punctuation wheels to practise a variety of punctuation marks.
- With a partner, take turns to spin a punctuation wheel and write a sentence or a phrase to include the form of punctuation that the wheel has revealed. (See page 4.)

Art and Display

Punctuation Palette

1. Divide two circles of white card into eight equal sections.
2. Using a chosen colour of paint, for example red, mix with white paint to make the tones progressively lighter.
3. Paint each segment of the circle in the tones from the original colour to the lightest colour.
4. Cut out and discard the last section or eighth of the painted circle.
5. On the second white circle, write one form of punctuation into each of the eight sections. Include commas, question marks, apostrophes for possession and apostrophes for contractions, full stops, capital letters, exclamation marks and so on.
6. Place the coloured wheel on top of the punctuation wheel and attach the two together through the centre with a paper fastener so that the colour wheel can be spun around on the punctuation wheel.
7. Cut out a large paint palette shape from thick card and paint it black.
8. Mount the colour wheels onto the paint palette using Velcro so that they can be removed and used by the children for language activities.
9. Use a large piece of cardboard and roll it into a cylinder shape to make a paintbrush. Add small drops of coloured card to simulate paint dripping from the brush.
10. Cover a display board in brightly coloured backing paper and attach the paint palette and brush to the display.

The Animals Went in Two by Two

Language Activities

Nouns – words that name a thing or a feeling.

- Read the story of Noah's Ark from various sources such as *Noah's Ark* (*Usborne Bible Tales*) by Heather Armery (Usborne Publishing Ltd, 1996). Choose suitable versions of the story as a basis to develop work on common, proper, collective and abstract nouns.

Common Nouns

Common noun – a non-specific reference to a thing such as *man, dog, shop*.

- Identify and list all the nouns or non-specific things featured in the story of Noah's Ark such as *ark, sea, earth, sons, wives, animals, flood, rain* and so on. Group the nouns into living and non-living.
- Draw a picture to illustrate the common nouns. Label each common noun on your picture.
- Many nouns that we use are of masculine or feminine gender such as *man*, *woman*, *son*, *daughter*, *cow*, *bull*, *cockerel*, *hen* and so on. List the animals featured in the story of Noah's Ark and using information texts research and list the correct terms for the male and female species of each animal.
- Find and list other male and female species of animal that may have entered the ark.
- Print out the male and female animal nouns on cards. Spread the cards out face down on the table and take turns to choose two cards to make a matching pair, for example *ram* and *ewe.*

Noun Stories

- Write your own short story related to an event in Noah's Ark. Perhaps one animal was not allowed into the ark or someone fell out. Use only masculine gender nouns.
- Highlight all the masculine gender nouns in your story and working with a partner ask them to rewrite the story using female gender nouns.
- Remember that all masculine pronouns such as *he*, *him*, *his* will also need changing to feminine pronouns.

Proper Nouns

Proper nouns – words that specifically name a person, place or thing: *John, France, Christmas*. Proper nouns start with capital letters.

- Identify the proper nouns from the story of Noah's Ark. For example *God, Noah, Shem, Ham, Japheth, Mount Ararat.*
- Rewrite a short paragraph from the story, replacing the proper nouns with pronouns such as *him, he, his, it.* Consider the effect that this has on the reader.
- Make up fun, fictional addresses for the characters and animals in Noah's Ark for example,

  The Dove
  1 The Treetops
  Flyaway
  Land Ahoy

Collective Nouns

Collective nouns – name a group of people or things such as *army, flock, crowd, gaggle*.

- Provide the children with a list of collective nouns for them to find the group of people or things named. For example: *bunch, plague, flock, litter, crowd, swarm, shoal, herd, army, team, pride, troop, gaggle* and so on.
- Can any collective nouns be used for more than one collection? For example, *a bunch of grapes, a bunch of keys, a bunch of bananas, a bunch of flowers.*
- Ask the children to find the collective nouns for the animals featured in the story.
- Invent new collective nouns for groups or collections of people or things such as butterflies, babies, trees and so on.

Abstract Nouns

Abstract nouns – words that name a concept or idea, such as *love, jealousy, hate*.

- In a circle, take turns to think of emotions perhaps experienced by the passengers on board the ark. List the examples: *hope, love, jealousy, hate, fear, faith, trust* and so on.
- Ask the children to write a sentence to suggest who might have experienced each emotion listed. For example: *Noah felt hopeful, he trusted God. Noah's wife felt anxious, she was concerned about the space.*

Art and Display

Two by Two

1. Make a Noah's Ark display featuring the male and female species of animals from the story.
2. Spray a mixture of ink and water onto blue display paper to create a rainy background. Use hand-held spray bottles to hold and spray the mixture.
3. Sponge the background of the ark using a mixture of orange and brown paint. Add detail to the thatched roof and wooden ark with a thick paintbrush in a contrasting colour.
4. Cut out pairs of animal shapes from thin card and use paints or collage materials such as wools, fur fabric, print wrapping paper, felt, feathers and so on to cover each pair.
5. Glue on moving eyes to add to the effect of each animal.
6. Position the pairs of animals together in the ark and label appropriately with their correct gender nouns.
7. Paint a rainbow on a separate piece of paper. Cut out and display the rainbow above the ark.
8. Finally, using a mixture of coloured corrugated card and transparent and clear coloured vinyl, create waves beneath the ark.

Very Important People

Proper Nouns

Proper nouns – words that specifically name a person, place or thing: *David, France, Easter*. Proper nouns always begin with a capital letter.

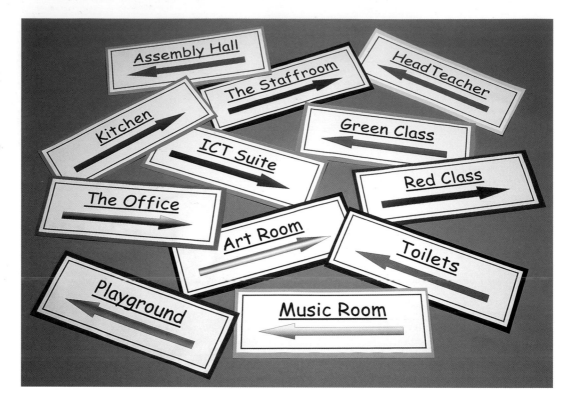

People

The Name Game

- Play a circle game to introduce the term *proper noun*. Sit in a circle and take turns to go around the circle introducing yourself using your proper noun or name. For example: *My name is Emily. Emily is a proper noun. I am an important person so my name begins with a capital letter.*
- Ask children to write their full name including their first, middle and surname. For example *Scott Alex Brown*.
- A person's initials also begin with capital letters. Write down the initials of each person in the class. How quickly can the children work out the names from the initials? For example *A. Ingham* becomes *A. I.* or *H. R. Nawaz* becomes *H. R. N.*
- Look in telephone directories to see how proper nouns are listed for names. Find and list ten proper nouns from the directory all having a different surname.

Places

Down Our Street

- Go for a walk in the local area and make a list of all the proper nouns that can be seen in place names, street names, shop names, business names, traffic signs, libraries, theatres, churches and so on. Do they all begin with a capital letter?

Very Important Directions

- Write down the names of all the rooms around the school building that a visitor may need to find such as The Staffroom, School Office, Hall, Cloakroom, Toilets, Kitchen, Class 1 and so on. Use a computer word package to make the names into large signs with arrows indicating the direction to follow in order to find each place around the school building.

A to Z of Countries

- Use an atlas to make an alphabetical list of the proper nouns used to name countries around the world. Try to find one country for each letter of the alphabet. For example *America, Brazil, Canada, Denmark* and so on.
- For five of the countries found above, use the atlas to name a city, a river and a mountain for each.

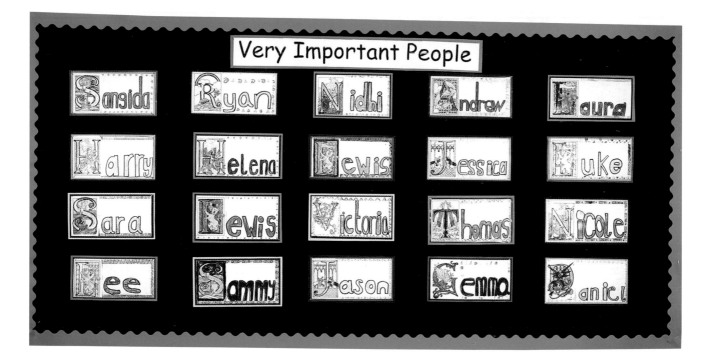

Things

Top Ten

- Make a list of your top ten favourite book titles. Note how book titles, and the author, publisher and illustrator names, all begin with capital letters because they are proper nouns.
- Collect all the titles together and present them in a class book called *A Good Read*.

Special Days

- Days of the week, months of the year and special holidays are all proper nouns that begin with a capital letter. For example *Monday, Wednesday, Sunday, April, May, December, Easter, Diwali, Hanukkah*.
- Ask each child to write a paragraph stating their full name and the day, month, year and place that they were born using a capital letter for each proper noun.
- Use diaries and calendars to make a list of special holidays and festivals celebrated throughout the year. For example, *Christmas, Easter, Diwali* and so on. Write a sentence stating in what month, and for whom if appropriate, each holiday is celebrated.
- Write a *School Year Book* for each calendar month. Include a short paragraph for each month with details of events, celebrations, visits and memorable occasions.

Art and Display

Illuminated Letters

1. Illustrate the importance of your own name by designing a name label with your own illuminated letter at the beginning.
2. Look at illuminated letters used in Bibles, fables and folklore storybooks. Identify the objects and decorations used in the pictures that surround each illuminated letter.
3. Ask the children to draw around a large capital letter stencil for the initial letter of their first name.
4. Draw and decorate the initial letter, perhaps with objects that begin with the same letter or items that are personal to themselves.
5. Use crayons, chalk or oil pastels to colour in the letter and the objects.
6. Glue the illuminated letter on to a rectangular piece of card approximately 30cm in length.
7. The children should write the rest of their first name on the card using a ruler for all straight edges.
8. Colour in and highlight each letter by tracing around the edges with a black crayon or thick pen.
9. Create a border of geometric shapes around the name to complete the presentation
10. Mount the names on a complimentary colour and display them in a uniform pattern on a black background.

Adjective Wall

Language Activities

Adjectives – words or phrases that are added or linked to a noun to describe or modify it. They may come before or after the noun.

Picture an Adjective

- Provide a range of pictures or photographs as stimuli. Pictures could include scenes such as woodland, a quayside, a waterfall, a colourful street scene or a festival.
- Identify and list all the nouns or people, places and things that can be seen in the pictures such as: *leaves, mist, fog, sunshine, boats, rocks, buildings, water.*
- Choose two or three nouns from the list and think of ways to describe them using several appropriate adjectives, for example *leaves – crispy, golden, damp, colourful.*
- Add more adjectives to the lists to create an adjective word bank for each picture. Print the adjectives onto card and arrange them around the pictures.

Circle Game

- Sit in a circle. Place an object such as a shell in the centre of the circle and take turns to describe the object using a suitable adjective. Watch the sentence grow. For example: *it is shiny, it is shiny, black and white, it is shiny, black, white and hard* and so on.
- Repeat the activity for other objects.

Let's Compare

- Compare two things such as two children or two objects. Consider how the adjectives describing the two things are made into their comparative forms by the addition of the suffix *-er*. For example, Lucy is *shorter* than Ben.
- Repeat the activity comparing three children or items and adding the suffix *-est* to each adjective. For example, Lucy is *short*, Ben is *shorter* but Sam is the *shortest*.
- Provide sets of objects, for example ornamental ducks, for the children to put in size order, from smallest to largest. Give them sets of comparative word cards to match with each object.
- Ask the children to make their own sets of comparative cards to put objects from around the classroom in size order.

Spelling Rules

- Compare adjectives that require the last consonant to be doubled. For example, *red, hot, sad* and so on.
- Identify spelling irregularities for adjectives ending in the letter *'y'*. For example *happy* becomes *happier*, *easy* becomes *easier*. Can you find other adjectives that follow this rule?
- Look at how the comparative and superlative forms are generated for adjectives, such as *beautiful*, *frightening* and *mysterious*.

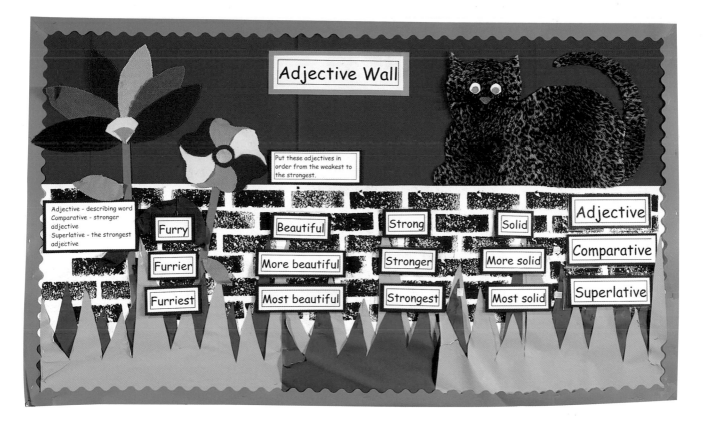

Super Adjectives

- Explore how comparatives and superlatives give strength to an adjective. Provide the children with a list of adjectives and ask them to change each adjective into their comparative and superlative forms. For example *dark, darker, darkest* and *hot, hotter, hottest*.
- Create an adjective wall to practise and display the adjectives, comparatives and superlatives in the correct order.
- Make up complex sentences using the adjectives, comparatives and superlatives on display.

Fact Finders

- Provide the children with a variety of information books. Ask them to find the answers to questions such as 'Can you find the world's longest river?', 'What is the name of the highest mountain?', 'Can you find the largest continent?'
- Choose your own information text and work in pairs to compose a series of comparative fact finder questions for other pairs of children to research.

Art and Display

Adjective Wall

1. Create an interactive Adjective Wall display to support the teaching of adjectives, comparatives and superlatives.
2. Use textured wallpaper to create the background for the wall.
3. Look at the textures and colours of building bricks and mix paint to the required colour to create a wall.
4. Use a large rectangular sponge to print a rectangular brick pattern onto the wall.
5. Draw a large cat to sit on the wall and collage with synthetic fur or material. Add moving eyes.
6. Use coloured card, tissue and felt to make flowers and grass and arrange these at the bottom and the sides of the wall.
7. Display the adjectives, comparatives and superlatives on the wall by attaching Velcro to the back of the word cards.

Express Yourself

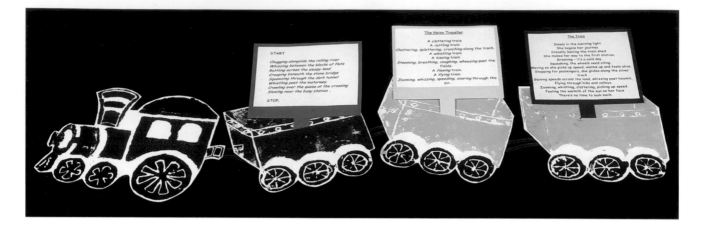

Language Activities

Adverbs – words or phrases that describe or modify a verb. Many adverbs have the suffix *-ly*: *happily, quickly, angrily.*

How Do You Do It?

- Make a list of adverbs to describe the manner in which an animal, person or object might move. Provide the verbs such as *dance, run, creep* and so on and ask the children to list the adverbs. For example a dancer might dance *agilely, beautifully, clumsily, daintily, excitedly, fantastically* and so on.
- Discuss how adverbs are used in a sentence to qualify the meanings of the verbs.

Locate and Position

- Compare the position of adverbs placed before and after the verb in a sentence. For example:
  The mouse quickly ran down the hole.   or   *Quickly, the mouse ran down the hole.*
- Read the sentence deleting the adverb and discuss the effect of its deletion. Was the sentence more interesting and informative when we knew how the mouse ran down the hole?
- Write your own sentences, changing the position of the adverb each time. For example:
  The monkey climbed up the tree skilfully.   *The monkey skilfully climbed up the tree.*
  The monkey climbed skilfully up the tree.   *Skilfully, the monkey climbed up the tree.*
- Discuss the effect this has on the meaning of the sentence and decide which one of these sentences you prefer and why.

Transport Poems

- Make a list of verbs and adverbs to describe the way in which forms of transport could move and sound. For example:
  A train-climbs up slowly, travels steadily, ascends gradually.
  An aeroplane glides smoothly, swiftly, quietly, stealthily.
  A motorbike stops abruptly, takes off suddenly, roars loudly.
- Ask each child to use verbs and adverbs to write a poem that describes the journey of one form of transport. For example:

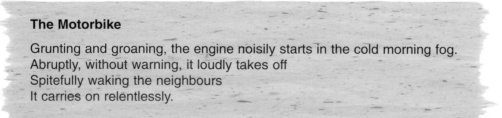

The Motorbike

Grunting and groaning, the engine noisily starts in the cold morning fog.
Abruptly, without warning, it loudly takes off
Spitefully waking the neighbours
It carries on relentlessly.

- Discuss the way the poem has been written and the way the reader's voice changes as the journey is described using the verbs and adverbs.

34

The Adverb Game

- You will need to make two sets of cards. One is a set of verbs such as *singing, walking, dancing* and the other is a set of adverb cards such as *quietly, noisily, happily, angrily*.
- Ask the children to choose a card from each set and act out the verb described by the adverb. For example *dance grumpily, walk happily, say the alphabet excitedly, sing a nursery rhyme frighteningly, or say the 2x table moodily*.

Parlour Game

- Play a revised version of the old parlour game 'The Minister's Cat'. Choose an animal such as a cat and use a dictionary and a thesaurus to find verbs and adverbs beginning with the same letter as the animal with which to describe it. When all possibilities have been exhausted, change the animal. For example,
  The minister's cat climbs curiously.
  The minister's cat crawls cautiously.
  The minister's cat creeps carefully.

Art and Display

Express Yourself

1. With a sharp pencil or a pen, press the shape of a train carriage onto a polystyrene tile.
2. Using primary colours, print several carriages onto thick cartridge paper.
3. Press the shape of a train engine carriage onto a polystyrene tile and print in red with a blue roof.
4. Press the shape of train wheels onto a polystyrene tile and print in blue beneath each carriage.
5. Arrange the engine and carriages on a display board and join the carriages together with pipe cleaners.
6. Illustrate each carriage with an adverb from the Transport Poems activity. Attach the adverbs to the carriages with self-adhesive putty. In this way, they can be regularly changed on the display.
7. Print a small engine carriage several times in primary colours, along the length of white border paper.
8. This idea can be repeated for different forms of transport and used to enhance story or poetry writing.

Intergalactic Connections

Language Activities

Conjunctions – words used to link sentences or clauses, or to connect words within the same phrase, such as *because, therefore, however, but, furthermore, additionally, later, earlier.* Conjunctions are a type of connective.

Conjunctions

- Share a piece of writing with the children that uses only the conjunctions '*and*' and '*and then*'. Ask the children what they notice about the writing and to suggest alternative words to link the sentences in the text.
- Make a list of the children's suggestions and add other alternatives to the list. For example *as, if, so, while, though, also, beside, which, since, first, second, even though, although, however, despite, meanwhile, yesterday, last week, later.*
- Ask the children to rewrite the text using a wider choice of conjunctions to join the sentences.

Connecting Clauses

- Model how to link two separate clauses, such as *I do not want to go to bed*, *I am really tired*, by inserting a conjunction between them. For example:

  *I do not want to go to bed **even though** I am really tired.*
  *I do not want to go to bed **although** I am really tired.*
  *I do not want to go to bed **but** I am really tired.*
  *I do not want to go to bed **until** I am really tired.*

- Make a list of the possible ways in which the two clauses can be connected and look at how the choice of conjunction can affect the meaning of the sentence.
- Provide pairs of sentences and ask the children to use a variety of conjunctions to join the sentences together. Explore how they can change the meaning of the sentence by their choice of connective.

Connecting from the Start

- Look at the possible positioning of connectives within a sentence. Place a connective at the beginning of a sentence to make it sound more interesting and show how a comma may need to be used after the first phrase. For example:

  ***Even though** I am tired, I do not want to go to bed.*

- Write your own sentences with the connective at the beginning of the sentence. Remember to add a comma after the first phrase.

Connectives – words or phrases used to link different parts of a text, such as clauses, sentences, paragraphs or chapters. Various words and phrases can function as connectives, for example *and, but, finally, also, furthermore, however, nevertheless, because, this means, just then*.

Sort Them Out

- Explore the variety of connectives used in different types of text, such as *narrative text, instructional text, reports, explanatory texts, persuasive texts* and *discursive texts*. Compare and contrast two styles of text by making a list of the connectives used.
- Ask the children to identify and sort the types of connective most typically used for each style of text and classify useful examples by: cause (*because, therefore, this means*); opposition (*however, but, nevertheless*); addition (*and, also, furthermore, additionally*); time (*later, earlier, just then, almost immediately, as soon as possible*).

Time Travel Stories

- Discuss the use of time connectives in story writing to show how time has moved on. Look through a variety of story books and make a list of connectives related to time. For example *today, yesterday, tomorrow, last week, last year, later, earlier, meanwhile, soon, before, after, since, once, just then, that night, at that time*.
- Write a short adventure story entitled *Intergalactic Connections in Space*. Include a variety of conjunctions and connectives to illustrate the passage of time.

Art and Display

Intergalactic Connections

1. Create a display board with the effect of space by painting swirls and stars with metallic paint on a purple background.
2. Marble white card in a combination of coloured inks.
3. Add setting gel to the inky water to restrict the movement and hold the shape of the patterns.
4. Create a feathered effect by combing through the marbling ink with a marbling comb or a rectangular piece of wood with small nails set in to it at approximately 5mm intervals.
5. When the card is dry, cut it into several spaceship shapes.
6. Decorate each spaceship individually using glitter, sequins, gummed shapes and pom-poms.
7. Position the spaceships randomly on the display board and attach conjunctions to the centre of each spaceship. Use self-adhesive putty or Velcro so that they can be regularly changed.

Spot the Ball

Prepositions – words describing the relationship between two nouns, pronouns, or a noun and a pronoun in a sentence. For example *on, under, between, for*. **A preposition is often placed before the noun to which it relates, such as,** *'The cat sat <u>on</u> the mat'*.

Nursery Rhyme Time

- Many prepositions are small words such as those written in nursery rhymes. For example *up, down, in, out, on, by, between, over, under, with.*
- Share a variety of nursery rhymes with the children and identify the prepositions used in each rhyme. For example:

  *Humpty Dumpty sat **on** a wall.*
  *There was an old woman who lived **in** a shoe.*
  *Jack and Jill went **up** the hill.*

- Identify the most common prepositions used in nursery rhymes.
- Choose one rhyme and illustrate the preposition. Compile the children's illustrations into a class book of prepositions.

Obstacle Course

- Create an obstacle course in the classroom, hall or playground using PE apparatus or classroom furniture.
- Work in pairs and ask the children to write instructions for their partner, explaining how to get from one place to another. Use as many prepositions as possible, taking your partner on a journey that includes travelling *over*, *under*, *in*, *around* and *between* objects.
- Ask your partner to underline the prepositions and to draw a diagram or plan of the journey as you have described it. Label the prepositions on the diagram.

In a Position to Play

- Choose a sporting activity such as football, rugby, netball or tennis and think of as many prepositions as possible to describe the position of the ball. For example *over, under, beside, in, out.*

- Use the list of prepositions to generate preposition phrases such as *in the net, over the crossbar, beside the line, through the posts, across the pitch.*

Antonym Prepositions

- Find appropriate antonyms for each preposition found from the sporting activity above. For example:
  under – over,
  on top – underneath,
  in – out,
  through – around,
  behind – in front,
  outside – offside.
- Use the computer to print each preposition onto large footballs to display.

Sports Broadcaster

- Imagine that you are a sports broadcaster, reporting live from a sporting event of your choice. Using the prepositions gathered, write a report as if you were at the event, and broadcast it on the radio.
- Write your report in the present tense and include as many prepositions as possible, for example:

  *And they're off. The horses are all in good spirits and the first to jump **over** the fence is Number 7, followed by 3 and 8. On **towards** the second hurdle. Oh, no, Number 4 has fallen **through** the fence. Numbers 1, 2 and 10 have fallen **on top** of her. What a catastrophe. As the others continue to move **around** the course, **past** the spectators' box, **beside** the lake and **over** the ditch, Number 5 begins to take the lead.*

- Read your report out to the class and ask them to count the number of prepositions that you have used.

Art and Display

Spot the Ball

1. Draw or copy an image of a person playing football or other sport.
2. Photocopy the image onto an overhead transparency and project the image onto white paper pinned to the wall to enlarge the figure.
3. Vary the distance of the projector to the wall to create images of different sizes.
4. Flip the transparency over and draw the figures facing in the opposite direction.
5. Cut out each enlarged image and paint the football figures complete with football strips of your choice.
6. Position the images on a green paper background on the display board.
7. Glue Velcro strips at different positions on the display paper ready to hold the antonym preposition footballs.
8. Make a goal using long cardboard tubes painted white and add string for the net.

Mini-Beast Mania

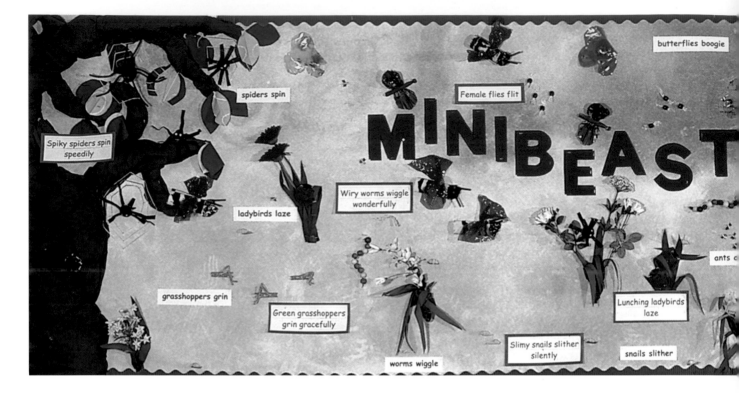

Language Activities

Alliteration – a phrase where adjacent or closely connected words begin with the same phoneme, for example *slithering snakes.*

Tongue Twisters

- Tongue Twisters are made from a sequence of alliterative words that are difficult to pronounce quickly and correctly. Find examples of tongue twisters to say together at speed, such as:
  Peter Piper picked a peck of pickled peppers.   *Around the rugged rocks the ragged boy ran.*
  Betty bought a bit of butter.   *She sells seashells on the seashore.*
  All I want is a proper pot of coffee.
- Highlight the words in each of the tongue twisters that begin with the same phoneme and discuss the humour and the sound effects created.
- Write your own tongue twisters, perhaps using your own name as a starting point.

Beastly Bugs

- Create alliterative phrases to describe a variety of mini-beasts. Begin with simple phrases that include a noun and a verb, such as *dragonflies dance, frogs frolic, bees buzz*, and build up the phrases to include adjectives and adverbs. For example, *dragonflies dart daintily, tiny tadpoles tango tenderly*. Provide dictionaries and thesauruses for help.
- Supplement the phrases with auxiliary verbs and prepositions such as *at, on, in, beside, over, under, behind, the, to.* For example, *beautiful butterflies bathing in a blue bowl, dragonflies daintily dancing in the desert, wiggly worms waving wildly in the washing up water.*
- Discuss the humorous effects created with the alliterative combinations of words and try to illustrate the phrases for display. (See Title Page.)
- Use alliteration to write a bug acrostic. For example:
  Slimey snails slithering
  Noiselessly in the night
  All along the alley way
  Inching onto icey islands
  Lazy, lolling, lonely.

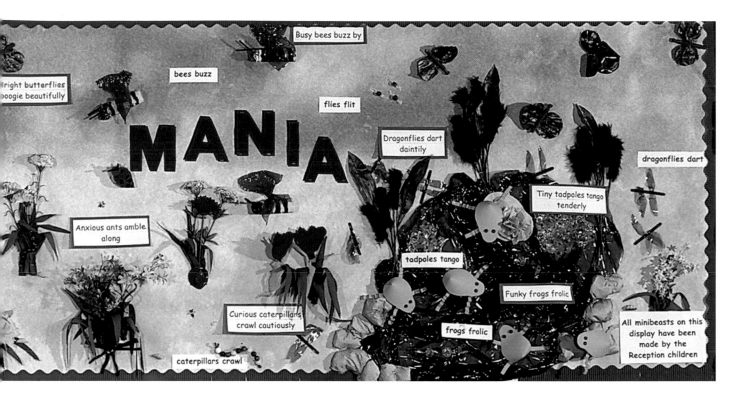

Art and Display

The Pond

1. Make a pond by cutting out a piece of green, transparent paper. Make frogspawn from large bubble wrap with a black painted dot in the centre of each bubble to represent the tadpole. Create bulrushes from rectangles of dark fur material. Attach a stem of green crêpe paper wound around an art straw.
2. Cut two oval shapes from green card for the body of a frog. Cut a two-centimetre slit into one end of the body, overlap and glue the two parts together. Make four small concertinas for the legs and glue them underneath the body. Add two eyes to the front of the head. (See Title Page.)

Flowers

1. Make daffodils by cutting strips of yellow crêpe paper into zigzag shapes and winding the strips loosely around two fingers. Remove the fingers and pinch out the zigzags at the top to make the petals. Add a stem made from green crêpe paper wound around an art straw. Make other flowers using the same method as for daffodils, but replace the zigzag strips with round-edged strips.
2. Make water lilies by cutting wide strips of pink crêpe paper into zigzag shapes. Repeat as for making daffodils to make four individual rosettes. Glue smaller rosettes inside larger ones and glue on to a circular piece of pink card.

Mini-Beasts

1. Make flies using large wooden beads with coloured net pushed through the centre hole for wings.
2. Make bees from yellow and black painted card tubes. Glue net wings in figure-of-eight shapes onto the back of the bees. Push black scrunched up tissue paper into one end of the tube to represent the head.
3. Cut coloured transparent paper into figure-of-eight shapes for the wings of butterflies. Concertina the wings and push into a dolly peg. Slightly fan out when secure.
4. Thread a selection of beads together to make caterpillars.
5. Glue pasta shells to pasta tubes to make snails.
6. Make ladybirds by cutting out a circle of red card. Draw a black line down the middle of this body piece. Cut a 2cm slit into one end of the body, overlap and glue the two parts together. Glue black spots on to the body and paint the head black. Add eyes and six black concertinas for the legs. (See Title Page.)

Word Art

Language Activities

Shape poems – poems in which the layout of the words reflects an aspect of the subject.

Share a Poem

- Share examples of shape poems from the book *Picture a Poem* by Gina Douthwaite (Red Fox, 1999).
- Cover up the titles of one of the shape poems. Read them with the children and ask them if they can guess the titles.
- Read the poem 'Sweet Tooth'. Ask the children why they think the last word 'tooth' has been illustrated in dark blocks.
- Can the children think of other ways to present Gina Douthwaite's poems?

Countdown

- Read the poem 'Countdown' by Steve Turner.
- Ask the children the following questions:

  - What shape is the poem written in?
  - Why do the words start with ten and decrease to nought?
  - Why is the poem about a rocket and not an astronaut?
  - Are the words real or nonsense words?
  - Is this a suitable shape to write this poem in?

- Write your own shape poem on a subject of your choice.

Countdown

Astroten
Astronine
Astroeight
Astroseven
Astrosix
Astrofive
Astrofour
Astrothree
Astrotwo
Astroone
ASTRO NOUGHT!
! ! ! ! ! ! ! !   ! ! ! ! ! ! ! !
! ! ! ! ! ! ! !   ! ! ! ! ! ! ! !
! ! ! ! ! ! ! !   ! ! ! ! ! ! ! !

Calligram – poem in which the formation of the letters or the font selected represents an aspect of the poem's subject. For example:

_{Little,} **Large** _{or} gr_{ow}th.

Calligrams

- Words can be written so they look like pictures of what they say. For example:

- Collect a variety of words that conjure up a visual image. For example *rain, sunshine, clock, rocket, lighthouse, thunder, wave, octopus, umbrella, steam, flowers, wheel, earthquake, volcano, candle, bell, star* and so on.
- Ask the children to select a word and draw the image as a calligram.
- Write a poem using one of the chosen subjects as a stimulus. Present the poem as a calligram using the font or letter formation to represent the subject of the poem.

Art and Display

Word Art

1. Draw an enlarged version of your chosen word onto cartridge paper.
2. Choose oil pastels for each letter in colours representative of the word. For example brown, orange and grey for pebbles or shells; blue, white and silver for clouds, rain and frost; and so on.
3. Glue small squares of sponge to the back of each word to give the impression of a 3D relief when pinned onto the background paper.
4. Prepare a background display board using pale blue backing paper sprayed with a mixture of ink and water (60% ink and 40% water) from hand-held spray bottles.
5. Mount each calligram on paper in a complementary colour and arrange them on the display board.

Stop, Look, Listen

Language Activities

Onomatopoeia – words that represent sounds associated with their meaning, such as *hiss, clang, crash, bang, pop, and whizz.*

Splodgely, Thlodgely, Plooph

- Read the poem 'Muddy Boots' by Philip Paddon, in *A World of Poetry* selected by Michael Rosen (Kingfisher Books, 1994). Discuss with the children what the poem is trying to tell us.
- Identify the use of nonsense onomatopoeic words in the poem to describe the mud.
- Most adverbs end in *-ly*. Using knowledge of adverb spelling patterns, consider if the words *splodgely* and *thlodgely* could be adverbs.
- The words in the last two lines of the poem, *'Scholdgely, Flopchely, Thlodgely, schrinkshely, slimy, grimy, squelchy, ghastly'*, are all adjectives. How do we know this?
- *Crispling* is a verb to describe the mud flaking off the boots. Can you find the phrase that helps us to identify *crispling* as a verb?
- Delete the muddy onomatopoeic words and replace them with adjectives, verbs and adverbs that make sense, such as *sticky, thick, glutinous, sloppy, dirty* and so on. Use a thesaurus to find appropriate muddy words.

Muddy Boots

Trudging down the country lane,
Splodgely thlodgely plooph,
Two foot deep in slimy mud.
Fallomph Polopf Gallooph.
Hopolosplodgely go your boots,
Slopthopy gruthalamie golumph.
Then you find firm ground again,
Plonky shlonky clonky.
BUT ... then you sink back in again,
Squelchy crathpally hodgle.

Sitting outside scraping your boots,
Sclapey gulapy criketty,
Cursing the horrible six inch sludge,
Scrapey flakey cakey.
Flakes of mud, crispling off the boots,
Crinkey splinky schlinkle.
Never again, will I venture into that
... Scholdgely, Flopchely, Thlodgely,
schrinkshely, slimy, grimy, squelchy, ghastly MUD!

Philip Paddon

We're Going on a Bear Hunt

- Read We're Going on a Bear Hunt by Michael Rosen (Walker Books, 1993).

- Identify the sounds to describe walking through the grass, river, mud and snowstorm.
- Substitute the onomatopoeic words in the story for your own new ones and read the story again.
- Repeat the activity, inventing nonsense onomatopoeic words for each obstacle in the story that has to be crossed. Describe the humorous effect created by the addition of these words.

Object Onomatopoeia

- Provide a variety of objects such as a kettle, a bell, a clock, leaves, a cork, chains, a firework. Think of onomatopoeic words that describe the sound of the objects and make a list for each.
- Invent nonsense onomatopoeic words of your own to add to the sounds.

Musical Sounds

- Provide a range of percussion instruments such as a tambourine, claves, a sliding whistle, shakers and a drum. Ask the children to play each of the instruments in turn and think of suitable onomatopoeic words to describe the sounds that they make.
- Write down onomatopoeic words for the sounds made by each instrument. For example, *The whistle goes whoooooooop! The shakers go sshhhhhhhooker! The tambourine goes ting, ting, ting!*
- Make sound cards for the instruments and display them together.

Art and Display

Now See Hear

1. Look at the use of onomatopoeia in the work of pop artist Roy Lichtenstein. Analyse and discuss his methods of taking printing techniques from newspapers and comic strips and recreating them using dots applied with a stencil brush over a paper which has been perforated with holes.
2. The words that appear in his paintings of comic strip characters sound almost silly, creating a sense of humour. For example *POW, VAROOM, BRATATATATA, WHAM.*
3. Choose your own onomatopoeic word to illustrate in the style of Lichtenstein.
4. Draw onomatopoeic explosion words freehand or using a letter stencil, on a sheet of paper.
5. Arrange the letters so they are as close to each other as possible or so that they slightly overlap.
6. Copy the word onto a transparency and use a projector to enlarge the word onto paper.
7. Draw two borders around the letters. Use a ruler if necessary.
8. Paint the letters red, the first border yellow and the second border black so that they depict and combine the colours used by Lichtenstein in his work.
9. Use masking tape to cover the straight borders so that the paint never overlaps.
10. Mount on red paper and cut around in a zigzag shape to give the effect of an explosion.
11. Display the explosion words on a yellow background splashed with red poster paint. Add a red border to the perimeter of the display board.

Lost in the Jungle

I have got black stripy lines
I've got black hair
I am a mammal
I am as fast as a horse.

What am I?

Language Activities

Riddles –
questions or
statements,
sometimes in
rhyme, which
form a puzzle
to be solved by
the reader.

What am I?

- Read the children a selection of riddles from *Jungle Animals (Silly Mixtures)* by Kay Barnes (Parragon, 2001).

Taller than most some would say
I reach for the sky both night and day
Head and shoulders above the rest
Orange brown patches around my chest.

What am I?

A Giraffe

- Solve the riddles by guessing the jungle animals from each description.
- Read the giraffe riddle and ask the children to identify the tense that the riddle is written in and in which person it is written. (First, second or third person.)
- When the last words of two lines of poetry rhyme, we call them rhyming couplets. Identify the rhyming couplets in the riddle.
- Read the riddle again and clap out the rhythm on each line.

'What's My Name?' Game

- Prepare a variety of opening lines for jungle animal riddles such as, *Spots have I though I'm not ill* or *My body markings are like a crossing on a busy road*. Print these on card and ask the children to match a picture of each animal with the appropriate characteristics described.
- Think of more jungle animals and their characteristics and ask the children to write opening first line statements to describe them. Use these as the basis for writing their own riddles.

Riddle Writing

- Choose a jungle animal and collect as many characteristics about that animal as you can to create your own riddle.
- Write the first line of your riddle and, using a rhyming dictionary, find words that rhyme with the last word of your line. For example, *Spots have I though I'm not ill*. The choice of rhyming words includes *kill, spill, till, will, pill* and *fill*.
- Use one of the rhyming words to help you compose the second line and continue this process for lines three and four.
- The rhythm in the first line of your riddle will determine the rhythm that you use. Try to keep the rhythm consistent throughout the riddle, although it does not matter if this is not possible.

Art and Display

Mask Making

1. Look at information books illustrating close-up images of the faces of wild animals.
2. Look at examples of real masks if possible and show how they are moulded to fit onto the face.
3. Practise drawing the face of an animal that will be made into a mask.
4. Tie and pin back all hair from the face.
5. Cover the entire face with the exclusion of the eyes, nose and mouth with Vaseline. This will prevent the material from sticking to the face.
6. The mask should take no more than 20 minutes to apply and, when removed, the face should immediately be cleaned.
7. Prepare the mod-roc and apply to the face of each child according to the safety procedures.
8. Decide which features will need to be added to the mask when it is dry, such as ears, nose, whiskers, feathers or beak. Using shaped card and masking tape, attach these to the mask. Cover in mod-roc and leave to dry.

9. Paint the mask using acrylic, oil-based paints or poster paints.
10. Varnish the finished masks with a mixture of PVA glue and water.
11. Finally, decorate the masks with feathers, sequins, strips of coloured felt and other suitable materials appropriate for the chosen animal.
12. Display the masks on an orange background and pattern it by randomly applying thick paintbrush marks in yellow and black all over. Attach seasonal foliage to the corners of the board to give a jungle/forest feel.
13. Position the animal riddles randomly on the board between the masks. Ask the children to read the riddles and match each mask to its description.

⚠ **Safety Note: For these masks, mod-roc or art-roc needs to be applied directly to the face. An adult should always apply the material to the face. Write letters to parents asking permission and explaining the procedure involved.**

Read All About It

Backdoor ban on hunting

Match the headlines to the pictures

GO ON! MAKE A RACKET

This chap's the cat's whiskers

Youths get to sail close to the wind

Take long walk and raise cash for endangered cat

MIND MEASURING

Language Activities

Headlines

- Collect a variety of current newspaper images, articles and headlines that will be of interest to the children.

- Cut out and display a selection of the headlines and attempt to predict what the story or article is about from the headlines provided.
- Ask the children to match the headlines to the pictures.

Snappy Headlines

- Notice how headlines are presented in a short and snappy style often with a play on words to attract the reader.
- Identify the use of contractions in headlines to keep them short. Consider which auxiliary verbs and prepositions have been deleted in order to contract each headline. For example: *are, has, can, been, on, to*.
- Rewrite headlines with the auxiliary verbs and prepositions in place. Read them out and discuss what effect this has on the reader.

Capital Headline

- Discuss the use of upper and lower case lettering in newspaper headlines. Look at several newspapers to see if there is a consistent pattern in how the headlines are written. Consider the effect that this has on the reader.

Writing a Headline

- Cover up the headlines on a variety of newspaper articles and read the articles with the children.
- Ask the children to summarise, in one sentence, the content of each article and compose a suitable headline.
- Compare the actual headlines used in the newspaper article with those composed by the children. Discuss the similarities and differences between the original and those the children have composed.

Photographic Headlines

- Provide a range of interesting photographs and magazine pictures from which to generate newspaper headlines. Choose examples that are powerful and will provoke imaginative headlines.
- In pairs, discuss the content of the images and create two very different headlines for the same picture.

Fairy Tale Headlines

- Provide the children with a list of popular fairy tales, such as *The Three Little Pigs*, *Little Red Riding Hood*, *The Gingerbread Man*, *Sleeping Beauty*, *Snow White and the Seven Dwarfs* and so on.
- Ask the children to write an eye-catching headline for each story.

Art and Display

Read All About It

1. Create a newspaper headline either by drawing freehand, using letter stencils or using a variety of fonts on a computer word processing package.
2. Ensure consistency in size and spacing between the letters.
3. Mount the headline on paper of a complementary colour to the letters and put on a newspaper backing.
4. Arrange the headlines on a display board and criss-cross string over the whole display to simulate a newspaper billboard or trim newspapers to use as borders around the perimeter of the display board.

Wish You Were Here

Language Activities

Evacuee Letters

- Visit the web sites of museums and galleries to find information and letters from children who were evacuated during the Second World War.
- Read the extract of a letter from Pam to her mummy and daddy dated 11th August 1944.
- Discuss the content of the letter to identify the style and time it was written. Consider the following questions:

  – Why do you think Pam wanted her fountain pen to be sent in the parcel?
  – What is an identity card used for?
  – Why do you think Pam bought so much soap?
  – What does Pam mean by her 'sweet ration'?
  – Pam went to a sale for the Overseas Mission. Can you find out about the Overseas Mission?
  – How much is 6d and 1/- in today's money, that Pam paid to get into the sale and to buy tea?

- Look at the structure and layout of Pam's letter. Identify some of the common elements of letter writing such as the writer's address at the top right-hand corner; the date beneath the address; the use of formal and informal greetings such as 'Dear' and the contents arranged in paragraphs.
- Identify the tense that the letter is written in.
- Can you find out why the letter was addressed 'c/o Mrs Every'?
- This page of the letter is written in four paragraphs. Continue the letter by writing another three paragraphs in the same style as Pam.
- Choose an appropriate informal greeting with which to end your letter.

---

c/o Mrs Every,
Littlecote
Exeter Rd,
Moreton Hamstead,
Devon.

11th August 1944.

Dear Mummy & Daddy,

Thank you for the parcel received this morning. I don't think you sent my fountain pen & my Red + identity card but it doesn't matter.

I am glad things were quieter. Today here is dull & cloudy so far but it is not 10.0.a.m. yet.

Yesterday morning we fetched the milk for Mrs Every & on our way I bought some soap – packet of rinso, bar of Fairy soap & a tablet of Lifebuoy Toilet. I also bought the rest of my sweet ration, some toothpaste & some mending stuff.

Yesterday afternoon we went to a sale for the Overseas Mission. It was 6d to go in & 1/- for tea but Mrs Every paid for that. I bought

a needlework box	3.6
unrationed soap	1.1
moth balls	1.0
play	.6
2 raffles	1.0
	7.1

Letter Writing

- Read books, look at old photographs and watch television programmes to imagine how it would feel to be away from home during this period in history. Gather knowledge and vocabulary appropriate to the era.
- Provide a set of historical objects to look at that would have been used by evacuated children, such as gas masks, identity cards, ration books and suitcases. Make notes from all sources in preparation for drafting, editing and writing your own evacuee letter.
- In the role of an evacuee, write an informal letter to your family, recounting what has happened to you. Use language and vocabulary appropriate to the time in history.
- Age the letters by placing them beneath a grill on the lowest heat for 1–2 minutes.

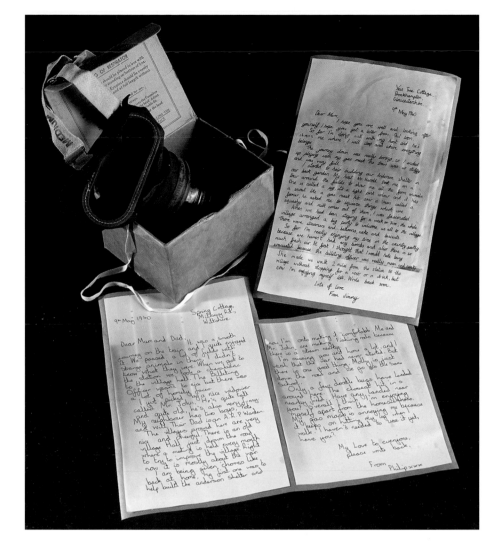

⚠ **Safety Note: An adult should always carry out the heating of the paper.**

Envelopes

- Collect a variety of envelopes delivered to your home. Encourage the children to bring in their own envelopes if they have received letters themselves and identify the elements common to envelope writing, such as writing the address in the middle of the envelope, indenting or blocking each line of the address, sticking a stamp in the top right hand corner.
- Write an envelope in which to send your evacuee letter home to your parents. Place your evacuee letter inside the envelope.

Parcel Tags

- On a parcel tag, write the address to which you will be evacuated on one side and the contents of your suitcase on the other side, such as a teddy, clothes, a stationery set, a photograph, a comb and so on.
- Add the parcel tag to the display board.

Art and Display

Wish You Were Here

1. Use a paintbrush to splash brown, black and white paint onto orange background display paper.
2. Enlarge and mount photographs of children being evacuated during the Second World War.
3. Enlarge and mount sections of the children's evacuee letters.
4. Arrange the letters, tags, photographs and envelopes on the display board.
5. Display primary sources such as gas masks, letters and photographs on a tabletop display in front of the display board.

Meals of Steel

Language Activities

The Iron Man

- Read the *Iron Man* by Ted Hughes (Faber Children's Books, 2001). Focus on chapters 2, 3 and 5 which vividly describe how the Iron Man eats metal objects as if they were 'delicacies'.
- Highlight words and phrases used in the text that help make the metal objects sound like very tasty food, such as: *chewed it like toffee, delicious delicacies, better than any spaghetti*.
- Identify and list the presents in Chapter 5 that were sent for the Iron Man to eat.

Metal Menus

- Look at a variety of restaurant menus with the children. Compare how the text is organised and note the heading titles used for each course: *Starter, Main Course and Dessert*. Identify the conventions of the layout and the choice available within each course.
- Following the conventions of menu writing, create a metal menu for the Iron Man.
- Present menus wrapped around tin cans or written in a circular format and glued onto old CD discs.
- Mount other menus on to silver doilies.

Starter
Chain-link spaghetti
or
Iron and copper fillets on
a crunchy bed of rocket

Main Course
Chargrilled toasters
or
Deep-fried door locks
with seasonal salad

Dessert
Sticky toffee cooker
and aluminium custard
or
Raspberry tools

Oil and after dinner iron filings

Metal Food

- Ask the children to list metal objects that they think the Iron Man would like to eat. For example *an iron, door locks, cutlery, cooker, washIng machIne, fridge, lawn mower, scissors* and so on.
- Decide how the metal food items could be combined with real food to make appetising food for the Iron Man, such as *chain-link spaghetti* or *lightly baked cooker with seafood sauce*.

Art and Display

The Iron Man

1. Trace or draw the body of the Iron Man.
2. Photocopy the body onto an overhead transparency and draw a life-size version by projecting the transparency onto a wall of silver card.
3. Remove the card from the wall and, using a black marker pen, highlight the joints.
4. Add shiny eyes cut out from metallic paper.
5. Attach the Iron Man to the display board and add green strips of paper in the shape of grass to the bottom of the board.
6. Cut out letters for 'The Iron Man' title from holographic or metallic paper.
7. Position the silver doily menus randomly on the display board.

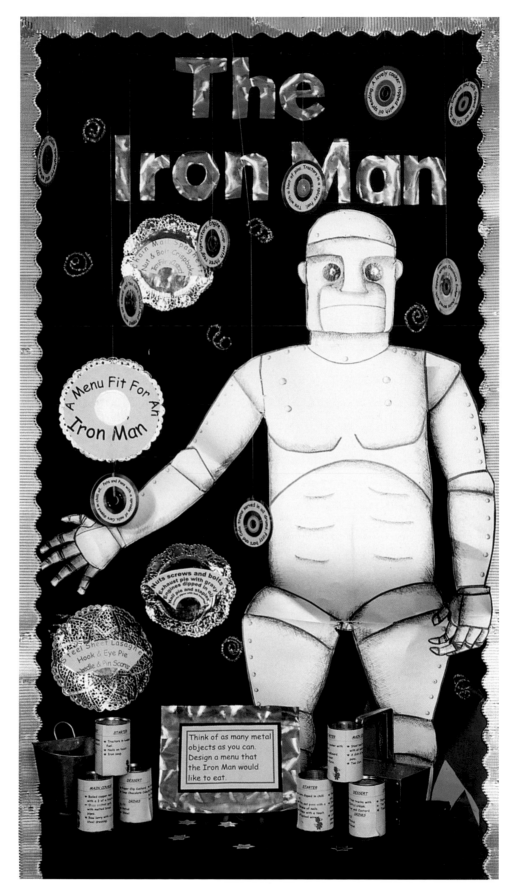

8. Suspend the CD menus from the ceiling so that they fall at different heights in front of the display board.
9. Cover a display table with black cloth and stack the tin can menus on the table.
10. Fill metal buckets and pots with chains and other metal objects and display these alongside the menus.

53

Food, Glorious Food

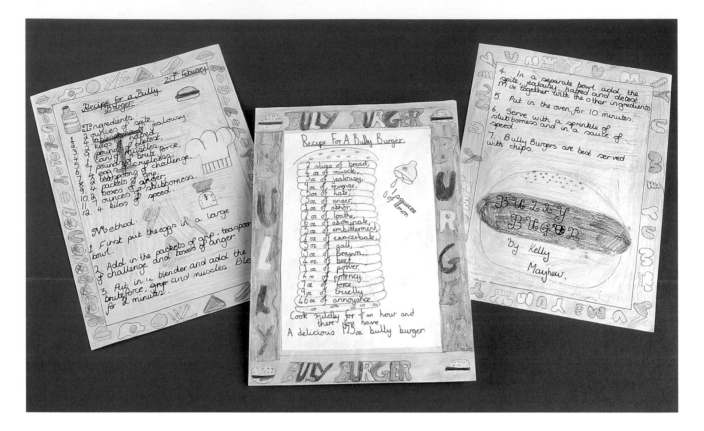

Language Activities

Recipes

- Collect a variety of recipes from books, recipe cards and magazines. Identify their distinguishing features such as the listing of ingredients, the sequence and organisation of each stage of the method, the commands used to introduce each stage.
- Compare how different recipe books use a variety of organisational devices in order to make the text easier to follow, for example lists, sub-headings, diagrams, bullet points, numbers or symbols.
- Consider why the ingredients are generally not numbered and discuss the reasons for using numbers or bullet points to list the method.
- Explain and discuss the terms *chronological* and *non-chronological order* and identify which parts of a recipe are chronological and non-chronological.
- Provide the method for a variety of recipes written in the wrong order and ask the children to rewrite the recipe in the correct chronological order.

Language of Commands

- Identify and list the imperative verbs used at the beginning of instructions to give commands. For example *mix, add, put, bake, roll, melt, pour.*
- Look at the position of the verb in the instructional sentences.
- Provide the children with recipe methods with the imperative verbs deleted and ask them to add an appropriate verb from the list to complete each sentence.

Following Instructions

- Read and follow simple instructions for making a jelly.
- Write your own simple instructions for making a sandwich. Use appropriate language and a variety of organisational devices.
- Draw diagrams to illustrate the instructions for making jelly and a sandwich, and if possible ask a partner to test them out.

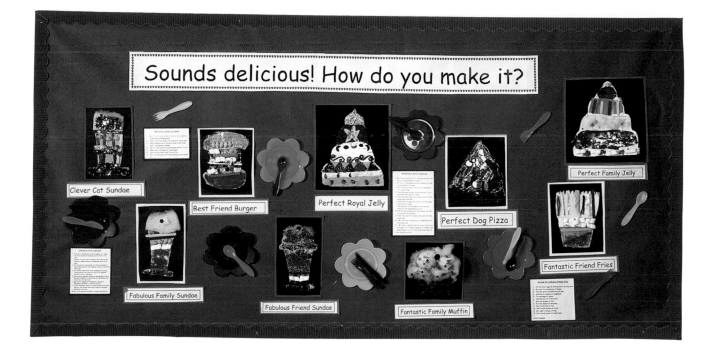

Fanciful Recipes

- Create a fanciful recipe for a perfect pet, fantastic friend, fabulous family or big bully. Include the ingredients and method for each recipe.
- Begin by making a list of suitable imperative verbs and abstract nouns that might be included in the recipe. For example: *Put in a dash of love, stir in a spoonful of trust and heat until all the anger has evaporated.*

Imperative Verbs	Abstract Nouns
Put	Love
Add	Care
Mix	Friendship
Cook	Laughter
Stir	Trust
Weigh	Spite
Bake	Hate
Cool	Anger
Heat	Stubbornness
Pour	Greed

- Write the recipe and include organisational devices to improve the clarity of the text for the reader.

Art and Display

Fanciful Foods

1. Use thick cardboard and cut out the shape of the fanciful foods to be made.
2. Collage the food shapes with a variety of materials such as buttons, beads, pasta shells, sand, sequins, ribbon, art straws, coloured tissue paper and coloured card.
3. Display the fanciful food collages alongside the recipes on a brightly coloured display board.
4. A selection of brightly coloured plastic crockery and cutlery could be arranged between the artwork to add further interest.

Best Friend Burger

Special Greetings

Language Activities

Haiku – a Japanese form of poetry constructed in 3 lines of 17 syllables in the pattern 5, 7, 5.

Haiku Poems

- Read the following haiku poems by John Cooper Clark and Roger Stevens, in *The Works* chosen by Paul Cookson (Macmillan Children's Books, 2000). Discuss the composition and play on words in the two poems.

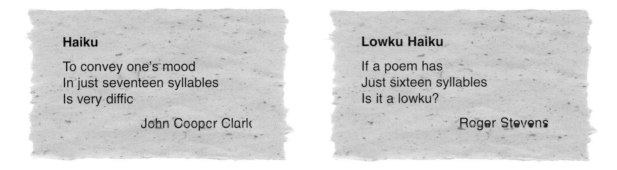

Haiku

To convey one's mood
In just seventeen syllables
Is very diffic

        John Cooper Clark

Lowku Haiku

If a poem has
Just sixteen syllables
Is it a lowku?

        Roger Stevens

- Why did the poet fail to complete the last word in the first Haiku poem?
- How many syllables does Roger Stevens use in his Haiku poem?
- Read the poems and ask the children to clap out the syllables in each word as they read. Are there any similarities between the two poems in terms of lines and syllables?
- How many syllables are there all together in each Haiku poem?

Haiku Greetings

- Create a list of themes for which haiku greetings could be written such as birthdays, leaving, thank you, sorry, friendship, Christmas, Easter and so on.
- Generate a list of suitable words that could be used to write a haiku for each of the themes. For example *Birthday (congratulations, celebrate), Leaving (sorry, miss you, good luck), Sorry (mistake, apologise), Friendship (forever, strong, best)* and so on.

- Think about the message, the mood and the feelings that you wish to convey in the haiku greetings, for example, a 'Sorry' haiku poem should try to tell the person how you feel about what has happened and should include words to help them feel better.
- Model how a possible haiku could be written for one of the special occasion themes. For example, for thank you:

  The present is great.   (5)
  I smiled when I opened it. (7)
  Thank you, once again.   (5)

- Write haiku greetings for a special occasion following the syllable pattern for each line.

Art and Display

Greetings Cards

Three Silver Hearts

1. Cut out three small squares of metallic embossing foil and, using a pen, draw a heart onto the back of each square.
2. Cut out three square windows from the front of a red greetings card and glue the foil squares on to the inside front cover so that they show through the cut-out windows.

Sailing Yachts

1. Cut out the geometric shapes for three yachts from metallic paper, corrugated paper and coloured card.
2. Stick the yachts on to black card with a sea of blue tissue paper beneath them.

Pink Flamingo

1. Cut out a pink flamingo and blue puddle shapes from card. Stick them on to a white background card.
2. Thread small pink beads onto a fine needle and sew them in two long lines through the front of the card to represent the legs. Secure the sewing firmly inside the card with tape.

Wire Butterfly

1. Mould very fine wire into a butterfly shape and thread small beads onto the bottom wings. Secure the wings by folding the wire back on itself.
2. Sew the butterfly in several places to a piece of natural coloured paper and sew the paper to coloured backing card using a complementary colour thread.

Red Star

1. Cut a red star from material or paper and glue it onto a square of cream material. Outline it using gold sealing wax or thick coloured glue.
2. Glue the cream square onto a square of black card and fix to a corrugated background card.

Blue Star

1. Cut out a small blue card star and glue it on to a square of corrugated card.
2. Mount the corrugated card on to a square of dark blue paper at angles to it and stick this to a piece of bright blue paper before gluing it on to a black background card.

Silver Star

1. Draw a star and write the word STAR onto the back of a piece of metallic embossing foil.
2. Glue the foil to a rectangle of gold sugar paper placed diagonally to it and stick this on to a rectangle of metallic gold tissue paper glued on a black card background.

Silver Heart

1. Sew a small silver heart or other type of bead onto the centre of a coloured square of felt material.
2. Use contrasting embroidery thread to sew the felt onto a square of natural material and sew or glue this onto a corrugated card background.

- Attach an inner layer of paper to the inside of each card on which to write or print the haiku greeting.

House For Sale

Language Activities

Persuasive Language

- Visit showrooms of new local housing developments and collect brochures that provide details of the building specifications, the area and the environment around the new development.
- Visit local estate agents and collect brochures and specifications of houses for sale.
- Look at and identify the style of writing used in the brochures to gain attention and to manipulate the reader, such as the use of bullet points, persuasive language, glossy photographs and artists' impressions.
- Photocopy and enlarge relevant sections of the brochures that use the most persuasive language. Ask the children to list the persuasive phrases that encourage you to want to buy the house. For example: *traditional pleasures, comfort and convenience, spoilt for choice, stylish modern living, superb kitchen, provides warmth and comfort, beautiful bathroom fittings* and so on.

Bias

- Read the brochures together and discuss the use of bias and half-truths, facts and opinions. Find examples in the text, such as: *We are one of the world's leading names in construction, Your superb kitchen is designed to look good and work hard, Your beautiful bathroom is stylish and functional.*
- Consider why developers write giving only their opinion of the houses and how this might present a biased viewpoint.
- What might be the effect of the persuasive writing on potential homebuyers?
- Which parts of the brochure specifically attracted your attention?
- Are there any parts of the brochure which you would like to change and why?

Writing to Persuade

- Take a walk around the local area and make a list of all positive aspects of the environment, such as *close to local shops and amenities, less than 2 miles to the nearest town, children's play park, community church, local schools, leisure centre, library* and so on.
- Look at the main selling features of your own home and list all the positive aspects. For example *three bedrooms, garage, gas central heating, double glazing, feature fireplace with gas fire, large garden* and so on.

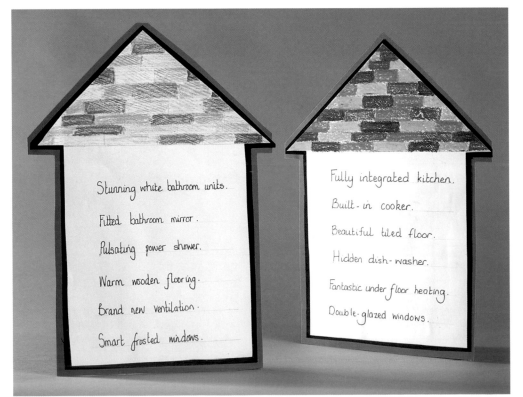

- As a property developer, prepare a brochure for selling your own house in your local area. Use persuasive language and concise descriptions to present the most positive aspects of your house or area.
- Present your writing on a large piece of paper cut in the shape of a house. Colour in the roof of the house with a suitable tile pattern.

Art and Display

House For Sale

1. Construct a large house-shaped background, the size of the display board, using white or cream textured wallpaper.
2. Using a rectangular sponge and brown paint, create a brick-like effect all over the house.
3. Sponge the roof brown.
4. Attach a fence made from corrugated card to the front of the house.
5. Intersperse the boards of the fence with flowers made from tissue paper and felt material.
6. Display the children's writing on the house-shaped background and position the clay houses between them using small tacks to hold them firmly in place.
7. Enlarge examples of persuasive phrases used by the children in their writing and intermingle these between the writing and art.

Clay Tile Houses (see page 2)

1. Draw a house outline on centimetre square paper.
2. Cut out and use the outline as a template for working with clay.
3. Roll out a square of terracotta clay about 2cm thick.
4. Place the template on top of the clay and cut around it to form a house-shaped tile.
5. Cut and shape smaller pieces of clay to make windows, doors and roofs.
6. Score each separate piece of clay with a blunt knife and score the house tile where the pieces will be attached.
7. Wet each separate piece and attach to the tile.
8. Use a pencil to make a hole at the top of the roof for hanging.
9. Fire in a kiln if possible or use self-drying clay if a kiln is not available.

A Fishy Tale

Language Activities

Adventure Stories

- Read *Kensuke's Kingdom* by Michael Morpurgo (Mammoth, 2000) or *South Sea Adventure, Underwater Adventure, Whale Adventure or Diving Adventure* by Willard Price (Red Fox, 1993).
- Look at the common features of an adventure story such as *a journey, conflicts, persuits, escapes, dangerous encounters, heroes* and so on.

Word Bank

- Generate words and ideas for an underwater adventure story plan.
- Collect the words under headings, for example: *animals, plants, landscape, objects, weather, sounds.*
- Make a list of possible problems and conflicts that could occur at sea to add to your story plan. For example: *bad weather overturns the boat, the compass is faulty, the radar breaks down,* and so on.

Fishy Consequences

- Play consequences as a different way of mapping out a story plan.
- Use only a few words that can later be elaborated when the story is written in its draft form.
- Provide each child with a piece of paper and read out a set of instructions such as those given below:

  1. *Write down the names of the three characters that will feature in the story.*
  2. *Write down a physical description of one of the characters.*
  3. *Write down how one character will react in an emergency.*
  4. *Explain how one character will react to good news.*
  5. *List the skills of one of the characters.*
  6. *State where and when the story is set.*
  7. *Briefly describe one problem or conflict that will happen in the story.*
  8. *Explain how the main character will change by the end of the story.*

- Following each instruction ask the children to fold over the paper to conceal their writing and pass the paper to the next child.
- The completed sheet of paper will become the story plan.

Deep Sea Scrolls

- Write the story plans on small pieces of brown wrapping paper to give the effect of old scrolls. Roll up each scroll and secure it with ribbon. Arrange the scrolls in the underwater story chest.
- Ask each child to choose a scroll from the chest, follow the plan and draft ideas for an adventure story based on the information given.

Art and Display

Underwater World

1. Cut out 2D shapes of fish, crabs and seahorses from thin card.
2. Roll very small balls of newspaper in a mixture of PVA glue and water, and fix onto both sides of the card. Add extra layers of paper to areas that need depth.
3. Cover the sea-life shapes with two layers of plain white paper coated in a mixture of PVA glue and water.
4. When dry, paint using acrylic paints mixed with PVA glue. This will prevent cracking and give a shiny finish.
5. Add details like scales and eyes using a fine felt-tipped pen.
6. Sponge-paint the inside of a large card box with blue, turquoise and purple paints.
7. Paint the seaweed shapes in PVA glue on the back of the box and sprinkle with coloured sand.
8. Cut out seaweed shapes from corrugated card, and stand on the bottom of the box.
9. Suspend the fish, crabs and seahorses from the top of the display box using transparent thread.
10. Make a story chest from a small card box. Cover the box in mod-roc and paint with brown and gold acrylic paints.
11. Place the story scrolls inside and around the chest.

61

Masquerade

Language Activities

Who Am I?

- Read the poem 'Who Am I?' with the children.
- Ask the children how the poem makes them feel?
- What kind of character impression does the writer of the poem give?
- Identify words and phrases that make the writer sound happy, sad, sensible or funny.
- Write down other characteristics to describe the writer.
- Discuss the effect of using the present tense in the poem.

Who Am I?

To my dad I am a growing child, someone to have a laugh with
And to share my hobbies with as I grow older.

To my mum I am someone to be proud of,
A helpful child who is becoming more independent as I grow up.

To my brother I am an older sister who gets on his nerves, but also
To mess around and play games with.

To my friends I am a quiet girl who minds my own business.
I can be funny, but I am usually sensible.

To my grandmother I am someone who listens to her happy memories,
Someone to kiss, cuddle and spoil.

Personal Word Bank

- Generate a list of words and phrases to describe yourself.
- Look at an old school report and highlight the words that your teacher has used to describe your school character.

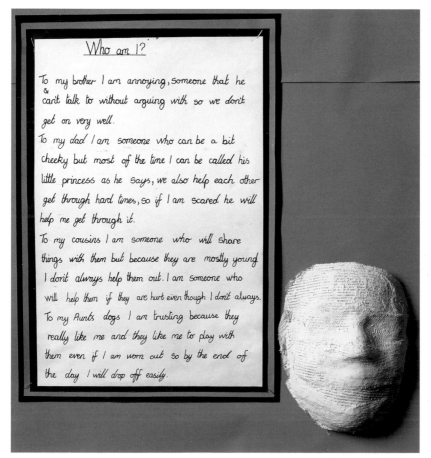

- Ask a friend and members of the family to compile a list of words to describe your character.
- Use your personal word bank to write a poem in the first person with the title 'Who Am I?' Dedicate each verse of the poem to your family and friends in turn, For example:

  To my brother, I am someone to help with homework and to share jokes with.
  To my mother, I am a shopping partner, someone who listens when she needs me.
  To my dog, I am a meal machine, a walking machine and a face to lick.

Performance Poetry

- Read and rehearse your poem and practise reciting it by heart.
- Perform your own poem to the rest of the class.
- Ask the audience to positively comment on the moods and character in each of the poems.

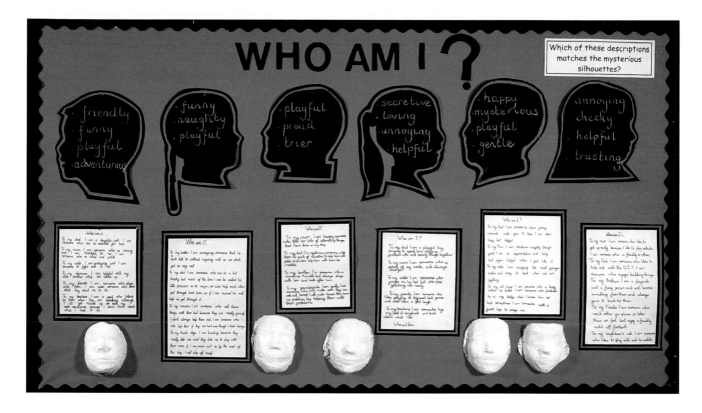

Art and Display

'Who Am I?' Masks

1. Tie and pin back all hair from the face.
2. Cover the entire face with the exclusion of the eyes, nose and mouth with Vaseline. This will prevent the material from sticking to the face.
3. The mask should take no more than 20 minutes to apply and, when removed, the face should be immediately cleaned.
4. Prepare the mod-roc and apply to the face according to the safety procedures. Apply at least four more layers.
5. Cover the mouth seconds before removing the whole mask from the face.
6. Place the mask over a balloon or a ball and patch up any holes before leaving to dry.
7. Display the masks on a table in front of the poems or position them between the 'Who Am I?' poems on a wall display.
8. Leave the masks unnamed and ask the children to match the poems to the masks. It is surprisingly easy to identify individuals from the mask profiles.

⚠ **Safety Note: For these masks, mod-roc or art-roc needs to be applied directly to the face. An adult should always apply the material to the face. Write letters to parents asking permission and explaining the procedure involved.**

Guatemalan Textiles

Language Activities

Artefacts

- Provide children with a variety of artefacts from a particular country or culture such as Guatemala, Africa or India. Pay particular attention to the use of colour, pattern and texture in the art, fabrics and clothing.
- Ask the children to choose one of the artefacts to describe to a friend.
- Write a report to describe your chosen artefact, for example:

The hat has a bumpy texture. I think it is very pretty and must be quite itchy to wear. The texture is smooth where the knitting is in lines. I can see primary and secondary colours woven together. I think that they must have been made from natural dyes. The pattern repeats itself. I can see lots of geometric shapes.

Art Exhibitio n

- Plan and organise a classroom exhibition of Guatemalan art produced by the children in Art and Display.
- Create a list of factual information about your chosen piece of work to be included in a catalogue for visitors who attend the exhibition.
- Write a description of your chosen piece of work to feature in the catalogue. Write in the past and passive tense, for example:

This work was produced using colourful crayons. (Past tense).
The work has been produced using complementary coloured threads. (Passive tense)

- Give your selected piece of artwork a title or name.
- Write a short description in the present tense about yourself, the artist.
- Take photographs of the chosen work using a digital camera, and add the images to a word-processed edition of each article for the catalogue.
- Design complementary posters and entry tickets using a computer PowerPoint package. List the important information that needs to be included on tickets and posters such as date, time, and venue, cost and content. Display the posters in prominent positions around the school to advertise the art exhibition.

Art and Display

Crayon Wash Designs

1. Look at a variety of Guatemalan textiles and identify the patterns, colours and shapes used in the embroidery.
2. On rectangular white card, draw a series of horizontal parallel lines.
3. On each line, draw geometric shapes such as rectangles, triangles and squares.
4. Colour in the entire card with colourful crayons.
5. With a large dry paintbrush, wash over the card with an ink and water mixture. Wipe away any excess liquid immediately with a dry cloth.

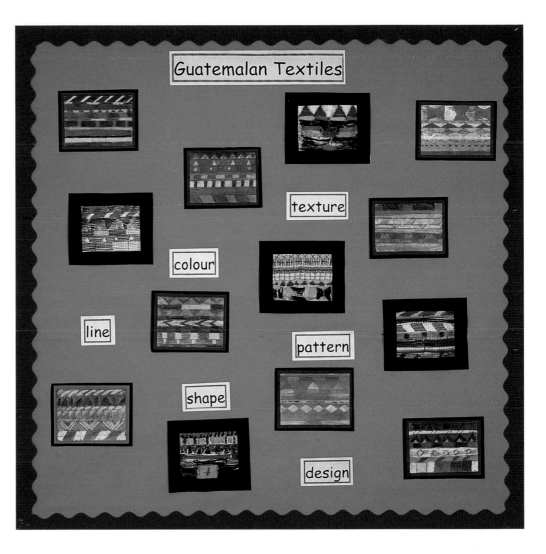

Fabric Designs

1. Copy the crayon design onto a square of Binca material, slightly larger than the rectangular card.
2. Use satin stitch and bright coloured thread to sew on the geometric pattern.
3. Glue a piece of card onto the back of the material to secure the threads.
4. Cut out a black card picture frame and frame the finished fabric design.
5. Display the fabric and the crayon wash designs together on a brightly coloured background.
6. Intermingle words to describe the artistic features of the work such as *line, pattern, shape, colour, texture* and *design*.

Flower Power

Language Activities

Contents and Index

- Use the contents pages of information texts on flowering plants to quickly locate chapters or pages on *pollination, seeds, fruits* and *photosynthesis*.
- Consider the reasons why the contents are listed numerically rather than alphabetically.
- Make your own contents page for a subject of your choice. Group the contents into subheadings. For example a contents page about bicycles may have the subheadings *Styles of Bike, Accessories, Cycle Routes.*
- Model how to use the index page of an information text. Ask the children to explain why single words in the index may be followed by more than one page number.
- Choose one word from the index which can be found on several pages and check each page to locate the word, discussing the context in which it is written.

Glossary Work

- Provide a range of information texts on flowering plants and locate the position of the glossary in each of the books.
- Compare how the glossary in each book is set out. Is it the same for all texts?
- Ask the children to identify the purpose of a glossary.
- Use the glossary of one information text to locate words and find the definitions for the parts of a flowering plant such as *anther, stamen, stigma, ovary, style, petal, stem* and *leaf*.
- Make your own glossary of words about flowering plants.

Illustrations and Annotations

- Use information texts on flowering plants to compare how plants and flowers are illustrated and annotated. Discuss the reasons for including pictures, flow charts and diagrams in information texts.
- Create your own flow chart to explain a process familiar to flowering plants.
- Provide flowers with prominent features such as Star Gazer Lilies or Daffodils. Look closely at one of the flowers and draw, label and annotate each of the organs.
- Write a small information book on flowering plants. Present the information using key words, headings, subheadings, illustrations and annotations.

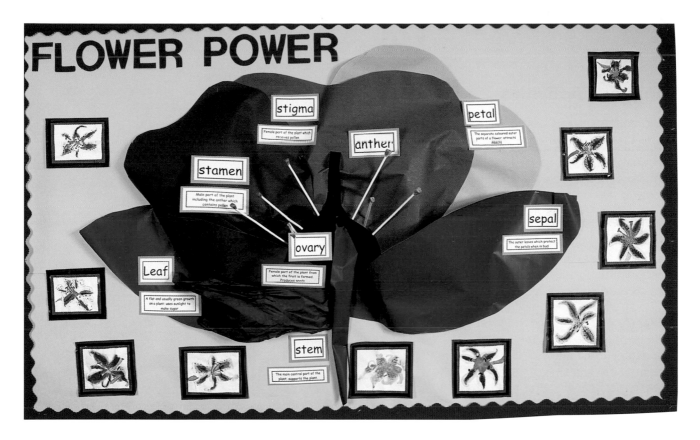

Art and Display

Flower Power

1. Make a large-scale flower by cutting out three large petals from shades of pink and purple paper.
2. Cut out an ovary shape from black paper, and a stem, sepals and leaves from green paper and assemble them together on the display board.
3. Create filaments from white straws and anthers from small polystyrene package fillers.
4. Colour the anthers with red chalk to represent pollen.
5. Computer print labels and annotations for the organs of the flower and position them in the correct places on the teaching display.
6. Arrange the painted flowers around the large-scale annotated flower.

Painted Flowers

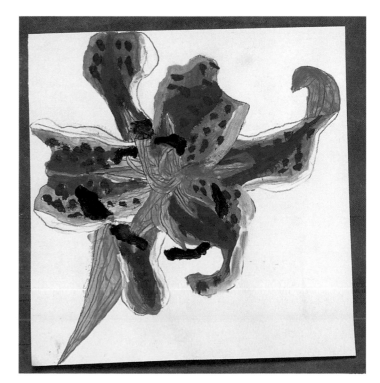

1. Use a variety of drawing pencils to draw the flower head of a Star Gazer Lily from direct observation.
2. Experiment with mixing the paints to match the colours on the petal, stem and leaves.
3. Using block or powder paints, model how to paint the flower, starting with a wash over the entire flower of the lightest colour, building up with darker colours until the very end when the darkest colour is used to add the finer details.
4. Paint the lily using very little water on the paintbrush in order to keep the colours strong.
5. Leave each colour to dry slightly before adding the next so that the colours do not blend too much.

Toy Shop

Language Activities

Instructions

- Provide examples of a variety of instructions, such as *game rules, how to make a model, how to look after a pet, how to use a household appliance, recipe instructions* and so on.
- Look at how the instructions are presented and collect ideas and examples of the organisational devices used to help the reader, such as lists, dashes, bullet points, numbered points, keys, headings, sub-headings and diagrams.
- Identify and list the connectives used in instructional texts to link sentences together. How many of them are time related? For example *firstly, secondly, earlier, later, next, after that, just then, almost immediately, as soon as, meanwhile, before, since, once, just then, at that time*.

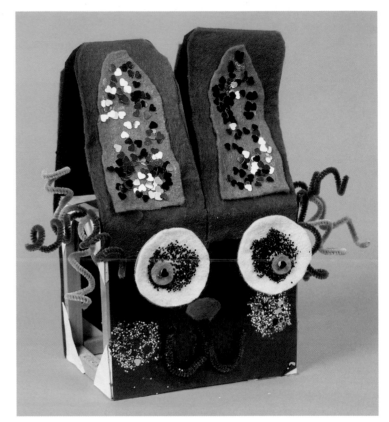

Chronological Order

- Look at the order in which instructions are presented. Are they in a chronological or non-chronological order?
- Write a list of instructions, such as *How to make a slice of toast,* in the wrong order and ask the children to rewrite it in the correct chronological order.
- Add other organisational devices, such as numbered points, headings and diagrams, to support the reading of the text.

Imperative Verbs

- Look at the examples of instructional texts and make a list of the imperative verbs often found at the beginning of the sentence to form a series of commands. For example *take, add, follow, turn, pour, twist, tighten* and *brush*.
- Provide a series of instructions with the imperative verbs deleted. For example *playing a game, making a model* or *planting seeds*. Ask the children to suggest an appropriate verb from the list to complete each sentence.

Writing Instructions

- Write instructions for making your model toy. Write the instructions in the past and passive tense using imperative verbs. Include time-related connectives to link your instructions together and incorporate any necessary organisational devices such as subheadings, numerical points and diagrams to support the reading of the text.

Art and Display

Model Toy

1. Make a 3D wooden frame approximately 16cm x 12cm x 8cm from lengths of softwood. Glue the frame together using PVA glue and add triangular corners to strengthen.
2. Cover the front and back of the wooden frame with coloured card.
3. Cut two pieces of dowel long enough to pass from the front to the back of the box and through the coloured card.
4. Mark the positions for the dowel to pass through the card at the front and back of the box and pierce the card with a sharp point.
5. Push the dowel through the card and thread a wooden pulley onto each piece of dowel, inside the box.

6. Test to see that the pulleys work by placing an elastic band around them so that when the dowel is turned, the pulleys move in the same direction.
7. Remove the elastic band and reposition it in a figure of eight around the pulleys so that when the dowel is turned, the pulleys move in opposite directions.
8. Place a cardboard wheel on each piece of dowel at the front of the wooden framework to represent eyes.
9. Decorate the front of the card with suitable materials to create the face of a character such as a rabbit or a tiger.

Christmas Verse

Language Activities

Kennings – words or expressions which describe something without using its name, for example *mouse catcher = cat*. A poem made of kennings would be a list of such expressions about one subject.

Kennings

- Choose a familiar theme such as pets or babies. Without writing the word *baby*, make a list of all things that babies do, for example *drink milk, dirty nappies, cry, crawl, giggle* and so on.
- Ask each child to write one expression or kenning to describe a baby from the ideas on the list. Collect together the children's expressions and use them to model how to write a kenning poem (see below).
- Discuss the humour that can be created through the choice of expression and explore how the words have been manipulated to conceal the object.

Kenning Poems

- Collect a list of things associated with a pet such as a dog. For example, a dog *wags its tail, licks faces, eats food from the floor, loves to walk, chases cats, barks madly, growls fiercely* and so on.

Milk suckers
Nappy fillers
Night bawlers
Carpet crawlers,
Food throwers,
Giggle boxes
Bundles of joy!

Star
Night compass
Sparkling jewel
Navigator
Distant eye

Father Christmas
Gift Bringer
Plump man in red
Vision in a sledge
Jolly, happy Santa Claus

Stable
Birth place of Jesus
Cradle for a bed
Warm, cosy house
Home to animals

Snowflake
Soft cotton wool
Icy confetti
Frozen water
Intricate lacework

- From the list, ask the children to select four or five expressions to put together a kenning poem about dogs.
- Working in pairs, ask the children to write their own kenning poem on a chosen subject such as cats, music, skeletons, food, computers, trains, for the rest of the class to guess the object.

Christmas Kennings

- Make a list of words associated with Christmas. This may focus on the Christmas story or be the commercial aspects of Christmas. For example: *Jesus, God, Mary, angels, stars, wise men, shepherds, cards, presents, tree, carols, Santa, stockings, parties.*
- Use your ideas to compose your own Christmas kenning.
- Print out the kennings on the computer and mount them on silver doilies cut into the shape of stars.
- Display the kennings on a table amongst an assortment of Christmas decorations.

Art and Display

Kenning Advent Calendar

1. Cut out two large Christmas tree shapes from card. Alternatives to Christmas tree shapes could be Christmas baubles, presents, stars or reindeers.
2. Collect fabric, paper, sequins, ribbon, buttons, beads, sand and glitter in co-ordinating colours such as shades of purple and silver.
3. Work horizontally across one tree, building up the layers of colour from top to bottom. Think carefully about positioning different textures next to each other.

4. Position and cut 25 square flaps through the decorated tree.

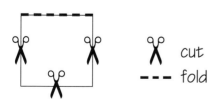

X cut

--- fold

5. Make a fold at the top of the three cuts.
6. Position the second card tree behind the decorated tree. Lift the flaps of the decorated tree and draw the outline of the squares onto the card tree behind.
7. Glue 25 of the Christmas kennings onto the marked positions on the blank card tree.
8. Glue around the edges of the decorated tree and reposition it on top of the kenning tree. Glue the two trees firmly together to make a kenning advent calendar.
9. Display the kenning advent calendar on a complementary coloured display board and decorate with icicle borders and paper snowflakes.
10. Open the advent calendar on the days leading up to Christmas and read out each child's Christmas kenning poem underneath.